In the Middle of This Road We Call Our Life

In the Middle of This Road We Call Our Life

The Courage to Search for Something More

JAMES W. JONES

Thorsons
An Imprint of HarperCollins*Publishers*

Thorsons
An Imprint of HarperCollins*Publishers*
77–85 Fulham Palace Road,
Hammersmith, London W6 8JB

First published in the USA by HarperSanFrancisco, 1995
First published in the UK by Thorsons 1995
1 3 5 7 9 10 8 6 4 2

A catalogue record for this book
is available from the British Library

ISBN 0 7225 3224 5

Printed in Great Britain by
HarperCollinsManufacturing Glasgow

For Emily and Carey

In the middle of this road we call our life
I found myself in a dark wood
With no clear path through.

DANTE ALIGHIERI
Divine Comedy, "Inferno"

CONTENTS

Making Connections

Do not believe that he who seeks to comfort you now lives untroubled among the simple and quiet words that sometimes do you good. His life has much difficulty and sadness and remains far behind yours. Were it otherwise he would never have been able to find those words.
RAINER MARIA RILKE

THE GOAL of childhood is to become an individual; the goal of adulthood is to give that individuality away. The task of childhood is to separate; the task of adulthood is to connect. This is a book about connecting; it is a book about love.

LIFE CAN be seen as a spiritual journey.

People come to me as a psychologist with various concerns: "I can't form meaningful relationships," "I feel stuck," "I'm getting depressed," "I'm fleeing into drugs and alcohol." While they wrestle with these complaints, other questions often emerge: "What do I want out of life, out of myself, out of relationships, out of work?" These are questions that can be answered only by exploring more deeply what gives energy and importance to our life, our friendships, our work.

People are looking for something and cannot seem to find it. They say they want more but cannot describe what that more is.

Many of us live disconnected from others, from parts of ourself, from a context in which our life might make sense. Many wonder whether their life matters in the larger scheme of things and whether there is any larger scheme of things anyway.

From innumerable psychic wrestling matches with countless patients and friends and with myself came a realization: What gives meaning to our life is being connected to something beyond our own ego.

This is an essentially spiritual experience.

Although there is plenty of talk in this culture about religion, most people tend to restrict religion to sabbath celebrations or an occasional holiday. Finding our life's meaning and purpose may appear to have little to do with creeds, rituals, or commandments. We therefore fail to see that the search for deeper connections, which echoes through our most intimate personal struggles, is essentially a spiritual quest.

The experience of connection to a greater reality that gives us meaning and purpose is the core of what I mean by spirituality as I use the term in the coming pages. In this sense our personal (and psychotherapeutic) struggles often require a spiritual solution.

The term *spiritual* may strike some readers as unnecessarily vague. Some may be more comfortable with more familiar and specific words like *religion*, *Judaism*, *Christianity*, *Buddhism*, *God*, or the *Holy Bible*. But this is a book for those committed to particular religious traditions and also for those outside any specific faith who still struggle with questions about what might provide meaning, value, and fulfillment in their life. Thus a general term seems more appropriate.

Also I am convinced that all religious traditions embody the experience of connection to a larger sacred reality. Without that experience, few of the teachings and practices of any religion make much sense. Religious services, for example, may give us a sense of tradition and may help us reaffirm that we are Jewish, Italian, Protestant, or whatever. But so can family parties and community festivals. Or religious teaching may provide us and our children with ethical guidance, but such guidance is also available from newspaper columnists and social commentators. What makes a ceremony or teaching "religious" or "spiritual" is its ability to put us in touch with a reality or presence or power beyond ourselves and our ordinary life.

In this book, spirituality will be discussed psychologically: The spiritual search involves discovering our true self. The result is a relationship with a larger, encompassing, sacred reality that gives our life meaning, value, and fulfillment. That is why the psychology of human relationships—which is a central theme of this book—is crucial for understanding spirituality.

But what keeps us from that relationship?

Another abiding struggle among many whom I know or with whom I work involves intimacy. This will surprise no one who reads newspapers or looks at the people around them or those portrayed in the media. People seem continually fighting to get into a relationship, out of one, or to improve one they're in. Whether it is with a spouse or a lover, a parent or a child, we appear to have increasing difficulty letting ourselves be known and finding others who are interested in disclosing themselves and knowing us.

Yet the drive for a more intense intimacy increases. All the sober warnings that such expectations are foolish and unrealistic fail to dissuade my clients, my friends, myself. Despite the pain that it often brings and the abuse of intimacy constantly paraded before our eyes, the longing to know and to be known wells up ever more powerfully within our heart and demands to be heard.

I have met men and women pounded into cynicism by loyalties betrayed and offers of self-giving refused. Others are numbed and depleted by the mindless routines into which they have sunk. Yet, time and time again, when that armor we have hammered out on the anvil of our own experiences is temporarily put aside, there is found a heart longing for others beating to the same rhythm. Driven into self-imposed isolation in order to survive the shattering of expectations raised once too often, or a barren childhood, or demands imposed without appreciation, still we dream of being more intimately connected to those around us. Many do not have a clear picture of what this connection would look and feel like; rather we experience only a faint sense of something nameless and unknown that is missing.

BECOMING INVOLVED with people who are only partially accessible has been a major pattern in my own life. When they withdrew, I was alone, thrown back on my own resources.

Like an athlete in training, I practiced being alone, making sure my survival skills remained sharp and ready, because isolation was the reality I knew at the deepest level of my being. We are essentially alone—this was the truth about life. Through several changes of career and two marital breakups, I learned that connections cannot be trusted. They are seductions designed to trap and weaken our ability to survive alone, an ability one must always have ready when these connections break as they inevitably do, an ability one must be constantly testing and strengthening. This was what I most deeply believed.

And it was a lie.

My life of chronically severed connections, in which I spent long periods living by myself, paralleled my inner sense that I was ultimately alone and that reality consisted of discrete and isolated atoms like myself. Perhaps this conjunction of inner and outer worlds was not coincidence. Perhaps my external life could not change until my deepest sensibility about myself and reality changed.

Such deeply rooted sensibilities are profoundly resistant to modification. They are beyond the reach of mere willpower or new additions to my system of beliefs. I cannot force myself to have a new outlook on life. Just telling myself I believe that I am not alone will do little good. Such transformations seem beyond the range of even the most intensive psychotherapy.

Psychology is not enough. At this level, change demands transforming my basic experience and vision of the way things are: experiencing myself as connected rather than isolated. Only from such experiences can a different and less fragmentary vision arise that might issue in a new life of trustworthy attachments.

Two COMMON concerns today: Does what we do and who we are have meaning? And how can we share ourselves and feel connected to another person or other persons? After years of working with people, it gradually dawned on me that these two issues—crucial to our well-being—are very similar. The same psychological issues are involved in both.

The heart of spirituality is relationship. Our experience with relationships shapes our encounter with what is sacred. Impediments to intimacy in our life are also barriers to spirituality. Giving ourself to someone or something beyond ourself requires trust and surrender. We fear trust and surrender because they appear to threaten us with the loss of ourself. Thus meaning and intimacy both come hard to us if they come at all. Often they elude us.

But if related forces are at work in our struggles with spirituality and with intimacy, the means of resolving them are also similar. Such is the theme of this book, which will describe some of the factors keeping us from intimacy and from spiritual experience and explore ways of rediscovering both.

I AM a clinical psychologist who is also a professor of religion, immersed both in the ancient spiritual traditions and in the troubled lives of contemporary men and women. I have spent much of my life reflecting on people's pain in light of the traditional wisdom of the human race and on the meaning of spirituality in terms of modern psychology. This book grows out of living at this intersection.

It grows also out of the experiences of many of my patients, a few of whose carefully disguised stories appear throughout. Please take the phrase "carefully disguised" very seriously. If you think you recognize any of these people, you don't. The illusion of recognition is only a tribute to the universality of human experience. Most of these accounts end in the middle, for these people's lives are not finished.

It is impossible to thank all the friends, students, and patients who have contributed in a multitude of ways over several years to this project. Their life experiences expanded my psychological and religious understandings. Their questions compelled me to think more deeply. Their comments continually provided new perspectives. They taught me, and this book is as much theirs as mine.

It is fitting that I dedicate this book on relationships to the two people with whom I have had the most continuous relationships, my daughters, Emily and Carey.

CHAPTER I

Is That All There Is?

Among all my patients in the second half of life—that is to say over thirty-five—there has not been one whose problem in the last resort was not that of finding a religious outlook on life.

CARL JUNG

THE MATURING mind becomes fascinated with more universal concerns. As life progresses, we generally accumulate a broadening spectrum of experience that requires of us more and more comprehensive ways of understanding ourselves. Thus studies of human development reveal a natural drive within us to make sense of our experience and a groping toward a more universal and encompassing vision. The struggle to find meaning by connecting or reconnecting with a universal, cosmic, moral, and sacred reality represents not a failure of nerve, the onset of premature senility, or a lapse into neurosis but is rather a natural part of the unhindered developmental process. The denial of this quest for the transcendent debilitates and impoverishes our life.

The sturdy fifty-year-old man, dressed in overalls and a red plaid flannel shirt, looked like he hadn't had a good night's sleep in weeks. As he sat across from me in my office, he was obviously uncomfortable.

"I can't believe I need a shrink," he said. "I just can't believe it."

"Maybe you don't, Ralph," I replied. "Can you tell me what's been happening?"

"I turned fifty this year, and things have really changed. My son Ralph junior is away at college, and my other boy, Stevie, has just gone into the service. My store is doing well—not making me a millionaire, but it's OK. And all of a sudden I start thinking, What does this mean? My life has turned out pretty much the way I wanted. Susan and I are happy. Oh yes, we have our fights, but who doesn't? Still, we're happier together than most people I know. My boys are doing well for themselves. My store is holding its own. But I keep asking myself, Is that all there is to life?

"So I go see my pastor, Reverend Harrison—I think you know him—and we talk and he tells me about having faith and it all sounds good, but I still have this question.

"Then, oh my God! I start dreaming of my tombstone—'Here lies Ralph, a good family man, a solid citizen, raised two sons, built a hardware store from nothing, coached Little League'—and I wonder all the more, Is this the sum total of my life? When I start thinking about my tombstone over and over again, Reverend Harrison says I'd better come and see you. He says maybe I have an 'obsessional neurosis' I think he called it. Am I crazy, Doc?"

After another interminable committee meeting at the university, I wanted to get out of the conference room as quickly as I could. I had appointments to keep, and the meeting had accomplished little. But Ben caught me on the way out. Ben was every inch the successful academic. His accomplishments were written up in the university paper on an average of once a month, or so it seemed. Not only was his research winning awards but he was president of his own genetic engineering firm, which was rumored to be making him a mint. Judging from the Porsche, which seemed oddly out of place in the faculty parking lot, the rumors were true. I knew him slightly because we had been on a couple of panels debating genetic engineering—the scientist and the ethicist, we had been billed—and now we were on this committee together.

"I'd like to talk to you," he said as we rushed out of the room together. We arranged to meet for lunch.

"I know this is going to sound crazy," he said from across the table, "but I'm really wondering about my work, and the questions I have sound philosophical and religious rather than scientific. Since that's your area, I thought I'd talk to you.

"I know as much as anyone and more than most about what the press calls the secret of life, how it probably arose, how it functions, how it might be modified. I know this gives us a tremendous potential for good, but recently I've started worrying about its potential for misuse. I tell myself that it's not my concern. It's up to politicians and technicians to decide what to do with the processes I've invented. But now I don't know. I think about what role science should play in the larger scheme of things, but I don't know how to answer that. I've been reading biographies of some of the men who worked on atomic physics, and they struggled with this too. But that's little comfort to me.

"If I just stick to the task at hand, the questions fade. But when I go home and look at my kids, I wonder what sort of world they will live in and what role my discoveries will have in making their lives better or worse. I know this is awfully trite. I tell myself everyone has these questions from time to time, but I just can't get them out of my head. Am I going crazy?"

In this culture we have made religion something optional, a leisure-time activity, another choice we have regarding what to do on Saturday or Sunday morning. Some choose to go to the movies, some to jog, some to enjoy the paper over eggs and coffee, some to attend synagogue or church—all options in the smorgasbord of contemporary life.

When I ask my students at the university to tell me what they think of when they hear the word *religion,* their answers almost invariably fall into two categories: things I must believe or rules I must obey. As long as we equate religion with creeds, rituals, or rules, religion is optional. It's my choice whether or not I recite the Apostles' Creed, keep kosher, or revere the Koran as the Word of God.

But there is another sense in which religion and spirituality are not optional, and that is the sense in which they are used in this book. Finding meaning and purpose is not optional; it is central to human life and is the goal of human development.

One of the joys of practicing psychology is watching the human life cycle. Working once in a hospital nursery as a psychology intern, I saw the fascination on the face of an infant as his developing mind began to discern a simple cause-effect connection: As he rattled his crib, the mobile above his head would shake. Later comes the mastery of language and the beginnings of the capacity for symbolism. The child learns that together the letters *b-o-x* stand for a box; as she plays, the box may, today, stand for a car and be played with accordingly; tomorrow it may stand for a house or a table.

But the child's world differs significantly from that of the adult. I remember once riding in the car with my preschool-age daughter and discussing whether or not the car in front of us was going faster. I insisted, with the consummate rationality of an adult, that since we were maintaining a constant space between us, the front car and ours were going the same speed. My daughter would hear none of it. Since the other car was ahead of us, it was going faster, period. In the world of the preschooler, the one who is ahead is going faster, and that's all there is to it, just as the taller person is always older. Because the child's thinking remains bound to the world of concrete, physical objects, the Swiss psychologist Jean Piaget calls this developmental stage "concrete operations."

Science, mathematics, poetry, and religion have their source in our capacity to become emancipated from the child's world of immediate experience. They require going beyond descriptions of physical objects to creating generalizations and using symbols. The child can see that 3 replicated 4 times yields 12, but a more developed intelligence is necessary to understand the ratio 12:3 as 4:1. That $2 + 2 = 4$ applies to apples, oranges, and planets; $E = MC^2$ is not an object in the world, but it is true of all objects in the world.

As the mind matures, it develops an increasing fascination with larger and larger questions and a widening curiosity about more and more universal relationships. The infant is struck by the connection between his waving arms and his spinning mobile. The young student suddenly grasps the process of classification and generalization and sees how dogs and cats and human beings can all be mammals, and a heap of loose sentences suddenly becomes for her a meaningful paragraph. The adult wonders about the meaning of loves turned sour and lives ended too soon and strives to sum up a heap of loose experiences into a meaningful life.

Ralph's curiosity about what his life added up to and Ben's concern about the moral meaning of his science were not lapses into irrationality but examples of human rationality pushed to its most developed levels. Having mastered multiplication tables and the meaning of grammar and then graduated into the challenges of raising children and/or forging a career, we naturally consider the more complex and provocative questions of the value and meaning of what we have done and who we have become.

The same trajectory appeared in the history of science. Many of the greatest physicists of the twentieth century spent the second half of their lives grappling with philosophy, ethics, and religion. For example, Erwin Schrödinger, in his essay *Mind and Matter*, covers the history of Western philosophy and religion in order to show how modern physics recovers what he calls "the mystical teaching of the identity of all minds with a supreme mind." In his autobiography, *Physics and Beyond*, Werner Heisenberg argues against the empiricist rejection of religion and goes on to discuss the relationship between his understanding of physics and the ideas of God and the soul. And Einstein, while rejecting traditional religious beliefs, continually affirmed the presence of mystery in the universe and the need for a "humble attitude of mind towards the grandeur of reason incarnate in existence which, at its profoundest depths, is inaccessible to man." These and other Nobel Prize winners devoted some of their most productive years trying to locate the theories of physics in a larger philosophical and moral context.

A vital part of human development is revealed in a concern with religion and the desire to find a framework in which life makes sense. My colleague Ben's maturity, rather than any psychological disorder, prompted him to struggle with the larger issues raised by the power of his science. If the struggle with these questions of meaning and purpose does not take place, and often it does not, our lives are impoverished. Religion is not a neurosis (as Freud thought) or the opiate of the oppressed masses (as Marx suggested). It is rooted in the dynamics of human development. As its drive for understanding matures, the mind increasingly seeks a more universal perspective from which to address the questions of life's meaning and purpose.

We need a language in which such questions can be discussed. Religious experience often clothes itself in particular stories of gods and heroes and overpowering events. The Lord of History appears to Moses in a burning bush. The god Krishna approaches his spokesman Arjuna in the midst of a battle. Athena and Zeus argue over the fate of the city of Troy. Such events and stories enable us to encounter the divine within the limits of our experience; they connect our particular world to the transcendent.

But we should not be misled into thinking that religious language is primarily particular stories like these. Religious language is essentially and necessarily universal. It seeks to express our most encompassing concerns and connections. Much of the paradox and difficulty of religion's speech must be understood in the context of religion's necessary but impossible task of using finite human words to speak of what might exist beyond the limited world that gave birth to those words.

Perhaps we could remain silent? The greatest philosopher of the twentieth century, Ludwig Wittgenstein, ends his *Tractatus* with the enigmatic injunction "Whereof one cannot speak, thereof one must be silent." But religious experience and the questions that drive us toward it propel us to try to speak of it. The medieval mystic Meister Eckehart spent his whole life insisting most vigorously that the divine is beyond words. But he could not keep silent. Famous as a preacher, Eckehart's collected works fill several library shelves! Whereas mathematics has recourse to the exceedingly abstract language of number and ratio, religion must try to free ordinary human language of its childish concreteness so it can be a vehicle for more universal insights and experiences.

Like all human activities, religion too develops and changes throughout life. A child's religion corresponds to his earliest concrete thought processes, when the capacity for abstraction and symbolization have hardly developed. Here religious language and ritual are taken with excruciating literalness. Children want to know how big God is, where "he" lives, and what "he" eats for breakfast. A recent popular children's book asks, "Does God have a Big Toe?" Childhood religiosity is also characterized by believing what you're told by some authority figure. Accepting things on authority is inevitable at this age because critical intellectual faculties have not yet developed.

With adolescence comes the capacity for critical thought. For some that precipitates a scrutiny of beliefs previously accepted on faith. Adolescence often represents the beginnings of personal autonomy and a natural resistance to simply accepting statements on the basis of authority. This adolescent period of upheaval and questioning is necessary in order to develop a faith of our own. During the earlier period of religious conformity, religious language retained a rather concrete and rote quality. Most adolescent criticism is properly directed against this literalism and the apparent absurdities that result from it.

Students at the university are quick to point out contradictions in the Bible ("Where," they ask, "did the sons of Adam get their wives?") or hypocrisies in the history of a religion (like the followers of Jesus or Buddha, who taught love and compassion, endorsing warfare). This finger-pointing at religion depends upon taking all religious stories and teachings very literally.

Much of that criticism loses its force with the capacity to tolerate ambiguity and the realization that religious language need not (and should not) be taken literally. Literal speech refers to objects in the physical world. God is not an object in the physical world. Acceptance of the ambiguity inherent in religion's attempt to speak about what is universal and transcendent ushers in a further stage of religious development.

At this point we may speak the formerly rejected language of faith, now shorn of the literalism that dogged our religion during our time of bondage to concrete operations. We understand that religious terms like *God*, *spirit*, and *eternal life* "point beyond themselves" (in the words of the Protestant theologian Paul Tillich) to a reality past the power of human speech to bind or encompass. There is nothing divine about the word *God*, but we may use it to express our relationship to the source of our life and its purpose. Adolescent questioning is not the final stage. Beyond it lies the possibility of reappropriating faith at a new level of understanding.

The same pattern of childhood faith, adolescent questioning, and mature reappropriation may be seen in our cultural as well as individual development. For example, the contemporary philosopher Paul Ricoeur describes three stages in the process of cultures coming to terms with symbols, myths, and meaning.

Originally there was only what Ricoeur calls the "first naïveté." This represents the mind untouched by science and philosophy. Religious symbols are simply assumed to refer concretely to events in the world of space and time: Adam and Eve were two people caught in an argument with a snake, and God is an old man sitting on a throne just beyond the reach of the latest space probe.

The natural and social sciences shattered the naive world of our ancestors and forever changed our vision of the universe. The earth no longer stood still at the center of the universe, and illness was no longer regarded as a sign of demonic possession. Now any college sophomore could declare the entire intellectual heritage of Western civilization bankrupt. Some religious spokesmen fight a rearguard action against modern culture and damn the last two hundred years of science and technology as a mistake. Ricoeur embraces the thrust of scientific criticism as necessary to free religion from the burden of trying to use concrete language to explain the inexplicable and describe the indescribable.

Unfortunately, however, Western society threw the proverbial baby out with the bathwater (as adolescents are wont to do). While justifiably jettisoning the literalistic forms in which religions had expressed themselves, modern culture lost touch with the experience of the ultimate and the question of life's purpose and value that those religious symbols embodied. Thus the criticism of religion is necessary to move beyond the spiritual equivalent of concrete operations, but it cannot be the final word.

Having passed through the baptism by fire represented by Darwin, Freud, Marx, Skinner, and others, modern Western culture (or at least some individuals within it) is ready for what Ricoeur calls the "second naïveté." Here religious symbols are reappropriated not to give us dubious information about the world of space and time but to point us to realities that elude those whose nets only troll the waters of the physical world.

The relentless rejection of religion that has defined modern Western culture is not the last word. Criticism frees religion from a misleading literalism and helps each person develop a faith of his or her own. However, such criticism is not the final stage of humanity, as the early prophets of modern culture thought. Actually it is more like the adolescence of the human species than its adulthood. And the turmoil of adolescence often obscures the fact that there are equally important developmental tasks to be done once adolescence is over.

Contemporary men and women are realizing that concerns about the meaning and value and purpose of their life do not disappear just because they have questioned, and perhaps rejected, authoritarian piety. The second naïveté is a rediscovery of those experiences of connection to a reality beyond the ordinary world of space and time that gives our life meaning and purpose. These experiences have often been lost in modern culture. Such a recovery of spiritual experience is a movement forward beyond modern culture and not a regression backward to authoritarian dogmatism.

For the last two hundred years, Western culture has been an experiment to test the hypothesis that human beings can be totally fulfilled in an atmosphere of secular rationalism, technological efficiency, and material abundance alone. Evidence for the falsity of the claim that we can live without meaning daily pours into psychotherapists' offices. We see the anomie and emptiness symptomatic of the present ethos with its disconnection from anything smacking of value, purpose, or the experience of the sacred.

In addition, contemporary psychological research into the importance of meaning and purpose in life demonstrates that without a sense that life is meaningful, people are more prone to anxiety, depression, and a variety of physical ailments. Studies have found that hope too is essential to physical and mental well-being and is a major ingredient in a person's resiliency in the face of crisis, illness, and suffering.

Hope, meaning, and purpose turn out to be critical for mental and physical health and for psychological strength and coping. Religion as their major source plays a crucial role in human well-being. As a purveyor of meaning, purpose, and hope, religion has a direct and documentably positive effect on mental and physical health. The quest for meaning and connection to the sacred is a fundamental part of human development and an essential resource for mental and physical wholeness.

These studies call the fundamental hypothesis of modern culture into question. Yet I hope these conclusions will comfort those who struggle with the search for meaning and purpose. So little cultural support exists for considering these questions that those who do may doubt their own sanity. However lonely this search may feel, it may well be part of a larger cultural attempt to move beyond the spiritually sterile atmosphere of our society.

The idea of moving beyond the modern outlook seems foreign, almost threatening, to many. I once presented a paper on the transition to a postmodern culture, sketching some of the themes discussed here, to an academic group and ended up feeling as if I were in the fiery furnace without my asbestos suit. Colleagues gave me hostile stares and made disgruntled comments during my lecture, and afterward several said they could not believe a scholar could entertain the idea of a transcendental reality beyond the ordinary world. Another time I asked a distinguished scholar lecturing on the history of the philosophy of religion if he could imagine history developing beyond the present period of critical rationalism. He said it was inconceivable.

This book is predicated on the claim that such a move is possible, even necessary. Critical reason is not the end point of human development but only a stage along the way. This is true for individuals; it may also be true for cultures. To rediscover parts of ourselves deeper than technical reason, to rediscover relationships with others that transcend atomistic individualism, to recover our connection with the sacred beyond secular rationalism—to make these connections is to move individually and collectively beyond the limitations of modern culture. The potential for this cultural shift, along with the pain expressed by so many of my patients because of their disconnection from any sense of meaning, gives this book its urgency.

Growing up, children may learn to speak of God, envisioning God within the limits of their cognitive frame perhaps as a giant man (or woman) who lives above the clouds in a great white palace. Children talk to their God as they do to their teddy bears, consulting "him" about the weighty matters of childhood.

But the time comes when children trudge off to school and leave behind the enchanted Eden of their private world. There they learn that beyond the clouds are only limitless curves of space bending back upon themselves: no great white palace, no friendly giant God, only the infinite, still emptiness. Gradually the child, now become a young man or woman, may cease to speak of God at all.

But perhaps one day, when staring into the face of his or her own newborn child, or when engulfed by the fierce beauty of the raging ocean or the soaring stillness of the mountains, or when confronted by the grave into which parents or friends have tumbled, or wrestling with recalcitrant fears and anxieties that leap unbidden from the caverns of the mind, the young man or woman, now become an adult, discovers that he or she has (in William James's words) "prematurely closed his accounts with reality" and that there is more to reality than can be dreamt of in any one philosophy. And the grown child may again speak of God, not as a giant in a palace beyond the clouds or a great policeman in the sky, but as a way of connecting with that sacred mystery that surrounds us.

CHAPTER 2

Discovering the Sacred

God speaks to us every day, only we don't know how to listen.

GANDHI

Or perhaps we don't know where to listen.

LEARNING REQUIRES doing. The beginning chemistry student is told to put water in a hydrolysis chamber, and she will see the water break down into hydrogen and oxygen. The beginning physics student is told to measure the rate of falling bodies and, if done correctly, finds they obey Newton's law of gravitation. Physics and chemistry involve practice as well as theory: Do this and you will learn that.

Science is a disciplined inquiry, demanding that its adherents spend long hours in the laboratory or at the computer terminal. Such sacrifices of time and energy are done in the faith that they will bring results. This is not blind faith; others have taken the journey of science before us and found it fruitful.

Spirituality too is both a theory and a practice. The word *experiment* and the word *experience* have the same root. Spirituality says, Do certain things and you will experience your connection with the sacred.

Like any disciplined search for knowledge, spirituality demands a sacrifice of time and energy in the faith that it will produce results. One of the reasons why the claims of spirituality may seem so unbelievable to us is that (unlike science) few in our culture have taken this journey, and so there are few to report on its results. Thus the spiritual quest often feels to us like blind faith.

Frequently the rewards of a journey are commensurate with the effort. The reward of viewing the world from the summit of a mountain, of standing where few have stood, comes only as the result of hard work. There are some places we will never see because we cannot or will not expend the energy to travel there. Some of us may never know the place within us where the sacred dwells because we do not undertake the journey there.

Connecting with others and with the sacred requires a different kind of training. It's not like learning to call an object a typewriter or coming to appreciate a poem or using a microscope correctly. Mastery of the multiplication tables or the intricacies of a carburetor is acquired impersonally. I can remain the same person and learn such technical information. Interpersonal and spiritual relationships, by contrast, will change me and expand my knowledge of myself.

A story is told in India about an argument among the gods over where to hide the secret of life so men and women would not find it.

Bury it under a mountain, one god suggested, they'll never find it there.

No, the others countered, one day they will find a way to dig up the mountain and uncover the secret of life.

Put it in the depths of the deepest ocean, another god suggested, it will be safe there.

No, said the others, some day humankind will find a way to travel to the depths of the ocean and will find it.

Put it inside them, another god said, men and women will never think of looking for it there.

All the gods agreed, and so it is said the gods hid the secret of life within us.

IF I TUNE two guitar strings to each other, one will vibrate when the other is struck—that is what it means to say they are in tune. Spirituality means tuning the spirit within us to its source. Sometimes people say that love means being on the same wavelength with another, that it means being in tune with the beloved. Jewish and Christian Scriptures say that we should "love the Lord our God with our whole heart and mind and soul." That could stand as a definition of spirituality. It is tuning our hearts to God, it is falling cosmically in love.

Being in tune with the sacred is possible because there is a pattern or image or point of connection between ourselves and the ultimate: There is a "string" that we can tune to God's vibration. Virtually all religions have said, in one way or another, that the image of God is within us. Because of the culture we grew up in, and perhaps because of the emotional defenses we have adopted, we may be unaware of that image of God within us. That divine pattern needs to be awakened in order for us to experience our connection with the sacred. Spirituality, like psychotherapy, is a process of making the unconscious conscious, of bringing into awareness the deepest recesses of ourselves where the divine dwells within us.

This claim that we are made in the image of God opens the Jewish and Christian Scriptures and can be found throughout the New Testament. The Gospel of John talks about the divine image within us by describing how the world was created in and through the "Word" of God, which is the "true light that enlightens everyone." The term translated here into English as "Word" is the term *logos*, which in Greek means the fundamental pattern or organizing principle that pervades each of us and the rest of the cosmos. The Gospel of John boldly identifies Jesus with this universal principle of truth and order. Christ is present throughout creation and within each of us.

The earliest theologians of the Christian faith (the so-called fathers of the church), who lived in the first few centuries of the Christian era, echoed the Gospel of John. In affirming the universal presence of Christ within the world and within each human being, they spoke of the *logos spermatikos*, a Greek term that means the seeds of divinity sown throughout creation and in the hearts of men and women.

The same idea can be found in the third century B.C. Jewish text called the Wisdom of Solomon. It speaks of the "wisdom of God" in a way similar to the ancient Greek use of the word *logos*. By the wisdom of God, this text says, the world was created. Then it identifies the wisdom of God with the Torah, or sacred teaching of Judaism, in much the same way as the Gospel of John identifies the logos with Jesus, indicating that the wisdom of God and the Torah are implicit in the order of nature and in our inner being. This idea was carried further by the Jewish philosopher Philo of Alexandria, who was a contemporary of the fathers of the Christian church.

This logos or divine seed or divine wisdom within us makes spirituality possible. Such a claim is not presented here as dogma to be believed but as a hypothesis to be tested by disciplined inquiry. Spirituality is that disciplined inquiry, it is experimenting with our consciousness to discover for ourselves the seeds of divinity within us.

Suppose for a moment it is true—and this is one thing virtually all the world's religions agree on—that there is within all of us a soul, spirit, atman, Buddha nature, or divine image, and that the purpose of life is to access and develop it. Each person must find for himself or herself the best channel of access and the best symbolic expression of it. The question of finding a spiritual path becomes, in part, To what can I give myself unreservedly? Dangerous? Yes, but equally dangerous is a life without ecstasy, without the numinous, without depth, breadth, passion, meaning, or purpose. Spirituality is process before content. Not memorizing rules, facts, or concepts but freeing the mind and the heart to explore new worlds of insight and connection.

Paradoxically such freedom is the result of discipline. I am only free to improvise on the piano after I have mastered the discipline of playing scales and chords. Likewise in order to gain freer access to the depths of the inner world, I must master the discipline of silence and learning to listen to myself in new ways.

Our inner world is often like our outer one—something of a chaos. If we try the simple experiment of attempting to be still and quiet, immediately a host of things comes to mind. We will probably be flooded with random thoughts, memories, emotions, images, and bodily sensations.

In order to let the depths of the inner world speak, we must be internally silent. But that is very hard to do. One way of facilitating that silence is to try not to suppress the forces that flood our minds. If we try to banish them, they usually fight back. Rather than squelching them, we can simply observe them. Not judge them, not fight with them, not approve or disapprove of them, but simply observe them as they pass through our mind. Saying to ourself such things as, Look, now I am thinking about what I must do for supper; now I am feeling angry at my child; now I am aware of a pain in my back; now I am worried about what I have scheduled for tomorrow.

If we can gradually put aside our natural tendency to evaluate and react to our thoughts and feelings and just observe them, we will find ourselves becoming increasingly detached from them and the observing part of ourself becoming stronger. Not that thoughts and feelings will stop—they won't. But they will not matter as much. When this starts to happen, a silence will begin to come into our mind.

In that silence, the still, small voice of God can begin to speak. And the deeper structures of the inner world can begin to come through. The still, small voice of God may come in a variety of forms—words, images, or pictures tinged with sacredness; states of serenity and oneness; memories and events seen in a new light. Meditation does not necessarily result in intense emotions but rather in interior states that are more encompassing and unifying than discrete ideas or feelings. This deeper reality will speak to us if we discipline ourself to make room for it.

If I walk into a university biology lab and peer through a microscope, I will see (in the words of William James) "a blooming, buzzing confusion." Where I see only a jumble of lines and shades, a trained biologist, by contrast, sees the fundamental structures of life, cell walls, mitochondria, chromosomes. If there is a discovery to be made on that slide, I will not make it. Part of learning biology is training our consciousness to see things we never noticed before.

Or in the physics lab, I may stumble on a bubble chamber photograph of a particle interaction. A physicist sees there the primal origins of matter. I see a beautiful configuration of lines and swirls that I might consider hanging on my wall because of its aesthetic elegance. If there is a new particle to be found among those twisting dotted lines, I will not find it. A physicist has trained his awareness to recognize things that I simply have no concept of and would never know to look for.

Spirituality too involves disciplining our awareness to experience things in a specially trained way. The student focusing all of her attention on a spiritually significant image of Jesus on the cross or the Virgin Mary or the Buddhist Bodhisattva of compassion; the Indian guru repeating a mantra or spiritually meaningful phrases in time to his breathing; the pious Catholic saying her rosary; the Christian repeating the words of the Lord's Prayer; the orthodox Jew listening to the echoing of the cry "Hear, O Israel, the Lord our God, the Lord is one"; the Eastern Orthodox monk using the Jesus Prayer ("Lord Jesus have mercy on me, a sinner") in time to the beating of his heart—are all disciplining their awareness and deepening their capacity for openness, receptivity, listening, and patient waiting.

The term *mantra* simply means "mind tool." It has nothing in particular to do with the religions of India but is simply a method the mind uses to train itself. Repeating the same image or idea over and over, especially when done in coordination with your breathing, causes your attention to become increasingly focused. There is nothing magical about the mantra itself, but a word or image that resonates with the sacred part of ourselves can bring that reality into our consciousness and into our lives.

The Jesus Prayer works much the same way. Repeating it can open up new vistas of forgiveness and acceptance. Dwelling on the Lord's Prayer and the petition "Thy kingdom come, thy will be done" can deepen our faith and trust. The mantra of Alcoholics Anonymous ("God, grant me the serenity to accept what I cannot change, the courage to change what I can, and the wisdom to know the difference") has helped many relax their grip on life. Concentrating on the majestic call "Hear, O Israel, the Lord our God, the Lord is one" induces profound states of awe and reverence.

Done mechanically, nothing will happen, just as merely memorizing formulas will not lead to an understanding of chemistry. A parrot can be trained to say the Lord's Prayer or a Latin, Hebrew, or Sanskrit phrase. But much of our life is a matter of what we attend to. Expanding the range and quality of our attention will bring real change into our lives.

LIFE INVOLVES continually shifting states of awareness. Right now I am aware of the typewriter in front of me. Earlier I remembered the pleasure I felt yesterday when I sat on the beach. Later on I will enjoy the caring and closeness of a friend. Along with these ordinary experiences, I can enter a state of awareness where I am conscious of being connected to a greater, spiritual reality.

Psychologists have discovered that what we know at any given time is a function of the state of consciousness we're in. This is called state specificity: Learning, memory, and cognitive processing are all specific to certain states of consciousness and may or may not transfer to other states. When you're depressed, you process new information and remember old information differently from when you're not depressed. In a hypnotic state, you experience the passing of time differently from when you're not in a hypnotic state. The state of consciousness you're in governs what stimuli you pay attention to, what kind of information you can learn, and what you can retrieve from memory.

Take, for example, our ordinary state of awareness, in which everything appears discrete. The table on which I am writing is a separate object, as is the friend who has just entered the room. Everything exists in its own physical space. Our culture overgeneralizes this type of experience, considering it the only reality. If the only reality is separateness and isolation, then there is no framework in which our life makes sense and has meaning. If we see ourselves only as fragments of matter, randomly and temporarily joined together, meaning will always elude us. Thus valueless, purposeless, violent images predominate in our media, loss of connection is endemic to our society, and therapists are kept busy.

To help students understand this, I sometimes do an exercise with them in which I ask them to relax, close their eyes, and imagine they live in a world empty of meaning or purpose, a psychological lunarscape, dead and bleak. I tell them, in this calm state, to concentrate on and to experience the feelings associated with the following images, which summarize the vision of reality taught by modern culture:

What looks like life is only the chance result of dead fragments coincidentally joined together.
What looks like meaningful order is but a myth imposed upon essentially random fluctuations of brute forces.
What feels like interactions between people are really only the effects of chemicals and electrons gliding through the central nervous system.

After allowing several minutes for this vision to have an impact on my students, I ask them to work together to organize a society based on this experience.

One group approaches clinical depression. The general lack of purpose does not motivate but rather discourages them. Unable to find anything meaningful or worthwhile to commit themselves to, they grow increasingly lethargic and apathetic. They picture themselves sitting in front of the TV for weeks on end or unable to get out of bed or taking stimulants to try to motivate themselves. Sometimes they see themselves eventually committing suicide.

Another group rushes into a frantic search for pleasure. They take more and more potent and exciting drugs. They change sex partners at a faster and faster pace. They drive powerful cars more and more recklessly. They live only for the pleasure and intensity of the moment. When asked to imagine where they would be after ten years of such a life, they cannot picture living a long life, and all see themselves as bored, burned out, or dead after a few years.

Unable to connect or work together, others explode into scenarios of violence or engage in brutal struggles to subjugate and overpower, in which one is a winner at best for a brief time until supplanted by the next wave of terrorists. They fantasize corporate takeovers requiring lies and deception and assassination, in which they amass large fortunes only to be taken over eventually by someone larger and more powerful.

Later the students discuss whether human life can flourish in an antiseptic and purposeless world.

Given the connection between states of consciousness and information processing, between the mental state we're in and the data that's available to us, *those aspects of the mind we allow to become active determine our picture of reality.* Our ordinary perception of ourselves and our world reflects our common state of awareness in which we attend to only certain aspects of experience—those seen as originating in the external world, those that fit our culture's preexisting concepts, those over which we can exert control. We exalt certain modes of knowing and types of knowledge—especially those associated with linear rationality and the control of nature—and devalue others.

If, along with the control of nature, our culture valued more gracious interpersonal relations or the cultivation of meaning or a sense of the sacredness of nature, we would honor other ways of knowing and states of consciousness besides linear reason. If the full range of our disciplined imagination, of our creative and intuitive powers, was engaged, a deeper and fuller reality would appear. This is probably what the contemporary psychologist and author James Hillman means when he says, "The gods are alive or dead according to the state of our soul." Sole reliance on detached observation and mechanical reason inevitably results in an impersonal vision of the world. Rational analysis alone is insufficient for a comprehensive understanding of our life. A disciplined inner life is the precondition for that more encompassing knowledge we call wisdom.

Recovering a disciplined spirituality is not a regression to irrational subjectivity. Meditation, honoring silence, focusing on spiritual imagery, uncovering deeper aspects of our nature move us past an uncritical reliance on critical rationality. Such practices relocate critical reason in a larger context and unite reason and intuition. They provide disciplined ways of shifting states of consciousness virtually at will, allowing us to move out of the detached mind-set that has dominated our culture and to enter that transforming psychological state from which spiritual renewal can emerge.

The picture of the world as composed of separate entities tracking their way through time is one, but only one, viewpoint. It is the best way to see things when I want to drive from one side of town to the other or to figure out how to get a billiard ball into the corner pocket. It is less useful when I want to discover if my life has meaning or purpose. Dealing with those kinds of questions requires a shift to another frame of reference.

In other states of awareness, things appear joined and interconnected. The conviction on which this book rests—a conviction that has grown stronger over many years of working with a variety of people—is that we are connected as well as disconnected. We are part of a reality greater than our individual selves.

An awareness of such interconnection is basic to many descriptions of spiritual experience. Consider three contemporary examples from three different people taken from a recently published anthology:

I came to a point where time and motion ceased . . . and I am absorbed in the Light of the Universe, in Reality glowing like a fire with the knowledge of itself, without ceasing to be one and myself, merged like a drop of quicksilver in the Whole, yet still separate as a grain of sand in the desert. The peace that passes all understand-

ing and the pulsating energy of creation are one in the centre in the midst of conditions where all opposites are reconciled.

And another's account,

Another experience happened to me . . . the evening of the day before my son was born. My first child had been still-born and, as I lay in bed, I was very anxious about my wife and much disturbed in mind. And then a great peace came over me. I was conscious of a lovely, unexplainable pattern in the whole texture of things, a pattern of which everyone and everything was a part; and weaving the pattern was a Power; and that Power was what we faintly call Love. I realized that we are not lonely atoms in a cold, unfriendly, indifferent universe, but that each of us is linked up in a rhythm, of which we may be unconscious, and which we can never really know, but to which we can submit ourselves trustfully and unreservedly.

And from a third person,

There came upon me a sense of exaltation, of immense joyousness, accompanied by or immediately followed by an intellectual illumination quite impossible to describe. Among other things, I did not merely come to believe, I saw that the universe was not composed of dead matter, but is, on the contrary, a living Presence. I became conscious in myself of eternal life. It was not a conviction that I would have eternal life but a consciousness that I possessed eternal life then. . . . The vision lasted a few seconds and was gone; but the memory of it and the sense of reality of it have remained during the quarter of a century which has since elapsed. . . . That view, that conviction, I may say that consciousness, has never, even during the periods of the deepest depression, been lost.

Experiences of unity and timelessness make us aware that we are part of something greater. Our relationship to this greater reality gives our life meaning and value. Such states of awareness are as much a part of our makeup as human beings as our perception of separation and disconnection is.

Since many of us have erected barriers against it, however, discovering that place of interconnection within—that "divine image"—may involve a deep, and often painful, journey of self-discovery.

CHAPTER 3

The Secret of Self-Discovery

Mary Ann was clear that she wanted help. She was overweight, stuck in a clerical job despite her B.A. in sociology, living alone, and her life was not working. She saw herself more as a problem to be solved than a person to be cared about.

She had seen numerous therapists—mechanics of the psyche who had given her tasks to do, books to read, skills to learn, and diets to follow. But she was still overweight, still in a dead-end job, still alone, and feeling more of a failure than ever since all these wonderful, time-tested treatments had not cured her. Despite years of practice, marathon weekend seminars, and hours of conversation, she still could not think positively, attract men, or keep out of the refrigerator.

She had long since given up on herself, on therapy, and on anything other than plain survival when we found ourselves standing in the same line at a reception following a university concert. We talked. She asked what I did and three days later called for an appointment.

"I don't believe you," she told me when I said I did not want to change her. "Isn't therapy about change?" she asked challengingly.

"No," I replied, "it's about acceptance."

"I don't understand. For a decade I've been trying to make myself acceptable by losing weight, learning to make witty conversation, and practicing an 'up' mood. I've read every self-help book as soon as it appeared on the shelves. I want to change."

"What were you thinking," I asked, "while reading all these self-improvement books and following all these suggestions?"

"I had to make myself acceptable," she responded. She stopped and thought for a while, then continued. "But every record of calories counted reminded me that I had to lose weight to be liked. Every self-improvement book just reiterated my need for improvement. Every trip to the therapist said to me that I was sick."

"No wonder diets went unfinished, self-improvement books piled up half-read on the shelves, and therapy appointments were canceled," I said. "Who wants to be constantly told that something is wrong with you and you need improvement like an old highway?"

She smiled slightly but said quickly, "But I still have to do something, I still have to learn to accept myself. God knows, I've tried that too." She said sadly, "It just doesn't work."

"Of course not. That's the contradiction. You're working on accepting yourself because you don't accept yourself. But working on it just reaffirms it. If you're being washed out to sea, all the swimming motions in the world are just going to tire you out and remind you that you're not getting anywhere."

"Then I'm really stuck," she said. "It's hopeless, there's nothing I can do."

Zen Buddhists tell a story about a monk who knew the secret of heaven and hell. A samurai went to see the monk, saying, "I want you to teach me the secret of heaven and hell."

The monk had been reading when the samurai arrived and didn't even look up. He simply asked the warrior curtly, "Who do you think you are?"

Deeply insulted, for he was easily identifiable by his splendid uniform, the samurai drew himself up to his full height and began to recite all his achievements.

When he finished, the monk again did not look up but simply turned and spit on the ground, a gesture of great insult.

Furious, the samurai drew his sword and was about to avenge the insult by running the monk through.

Suddenly the monk lifted his head and looked the great warrior straight in the eye and said, "Now the gates of hell are opening before you."

The samurai stopped short, frozen by the realization that his pride had overcome him. He dropped his sword and bowed his head.

"And now," the monk said quietly, "the gates of heaven are opening before you."

The monk knew the secret of heaven and hell because he knew how to create the experience of heaven and hell in his listeners. Likewise, the secret of self-discovery is found not in a book or a workshop or a psychological theory but rather by engaging in the *experience* of self-discovery.

One night when Mary Ann was returning from a weekend visit with her family, her anger struck her with such force that she could not drive. She recalled how she had been virtually pushed aside at the age of two when her brother was born. When she grew older, she was given almost total responsibility for him and was criticized rather than thanked for her work. She won scholarships and attended college, but no one from her family went to her graduation. In her mind she relived the scene of going back to her apartment alone after the ceremony and eating everything in sight. During the coming months she gained and gained until she couldn't recognize herself in the mirror. The more she ate, the more tired she felt. She remembered thinking that the grind of college had so depleted her that all she could do was take her honors degree and collapse into a clerical job at the university.

For weeks Mary Ann could do nothing in therapy but go over and over these episodes, her voice shaking with fury, as if she were trying to master them by sheer repetition. In the months that followed, she began to notice changes in herself. She was no longer as harsh with herself; she felt calmer; little things didn't get to her as much. Reflecting on her past attempts to change herself, she told me, "I lost weight sometimes but still saw myself as fat and ugly. I would make interesting conversation but still thought of myself as dull and boring. I joined clubs but felt lonely. I learned little and changed little.

"Over the last few months, I've been really furious, almost out of control, but in here I was still accepted. I was hurt, but you still understood. I was depleted, but I still felt strong. I didn't really learn to do anything new, but I saw myself in a different way. I realized I could be accepted and understood even when I was lashing out at everybody."

She was still overweight when she left therapy. Two years later I got a letter from Mary Ann. Only after leaving therapy was she able to go on a diet and lose weight, find the energy to start law school at night, meet a partner, and get married.

Self-discovery and self-acceptance, like the secret of heaven and hell, are not skills to be practiced but experiences to be discovered.

But where?

WITHIN EVEN the most disturbed personalities is a relatively healthy core: our real self, our true identity. Without access to it, self-acceptance, authentic intimacy, and mature spirituality are impossible. And the discovery of the real self requires putting aside the false selves we have developed throughout our life.

But how did we lose our real self behind a facade of false selfhood?

We enter the world totally dependent. We must receive before we can give. Food, protection, security, and affection are gifts in themselves; but, equally important, they are the source of our later ideas about what life will be like for us. If these needed supplies are given freely and graciously, we will learn to trust others and ourselves. If not, we will soon mistrust the world and either demand incessantly or lapse into passivity—or, at the most extreme, give up and die. The capacity to trust is one of the most important things we can learn as infants; it is the foundation of all later relationships.

Unlike the totally dependent infant, the young child can act as well as be acted upon. Now we can feed ourselves, pile blocks, manage crayons, begin to walk and talk, and use the toilet. Small achievements in themselves, but through them we learn more than a few simple tasks. We develop a sense of competency and discover how our activities are going to be received in the world. Watching parents in the children's ward of a hospital, I saw some who, with a gleam in their eye, warmly accepted their children's drawings while others just nodded at their children and returned to reading or conversing with adults.

As all parents know, young children are very lively. The typical two-year-old is into everything: overturning drawers, pulling pots and pans out of closets, mercilessly chasing the pet dog through the house. Families can support and appropriately channel that activity, teaching us to take initiative, or they can suppress it by being harsh and overly controlling. If our capacity for initiative is crushed, we may become so burdened with guilt that we cannot act forcefully. Instead we are frozen by the fear of retribution or of making a mistake.

Little Samuel could not do anything right. Everywhere he toddled he was pursued by a string of don'ts from his mother—"Don't touch that!" "Don't go into that room!" "Don't move so fast!" In junior high school, when he brought home a small bookshelf he had made in woodworking class, his father's only comment was, "When you painted, you missed a spot inside." In college his room was always the neatest in the dorm. His desk was immaculate, with pencils lined up in rows and notebooks stacked neatly on the side. One day a boy from down the hall found Samuel staring out the window, too depressed to move.

If our early activities meet with appreciation and encouragement, we gain confidence in our real self. If early accomplishments meet with rejection, criticism, indifference, or demands impossible to satisfy, we doubt ourselves. We may become rigid, precociously conscientious and meticulous, rebellious and defiant, or we may sink further into passivity. And we may associate relationships with being criticized or with feeling like a failure and learn to hide our real self as a condition of being in a relationship. Such feelings are the beginning of our false self.

Having tasted autonomy, the child toddles back to his or her parents to make sure that they are still there and that autonomy is not purchased at the price of the feared rejection or isolation. If his first attempts at autonomy bring rejection, the child must either regress back into infantile fusion so as not to be totally cut off or thrust himself forward into premature and fragile assertions of independence. In either case, the overly dependent and the overly rebellious lack the experience of autonomy that is the foundation of real selfhood and later intimacy. One collapses into dependency; the other is constantly in flight from it.

Taking in experiences is not enough; they must also be integrated into our developing sense of ourself. If early interactions are too tinged with pain, we may take them into our self but not incorporate them. They are swallowed whole and live on undigested in the psyche like Jonah in the belly of the whale, ready to be spewed forth at the first opportunity. These painful images of the rejecting, critical, unnurturing parent lie in our unconscious. From there these internalized but unacceptable images from the past are easily projected upon the present environment. Every teacher or boss becomes the controlling parent; every lover becomes the withholding or smothering mother.

The child who is neglected, rejected, or treated only as an extension of his or her parents feels rage and pain. To escape that pain, the child may comply with every parental whim out of fear of being rejected or blame himself for his parents' withdrawal and rejection. Thus we bury our true self to avoid punishment, criticism, or abandonment and take on the role of a dependent child or an evil person constantly on the verge of rejection. We will discuss later how religious language often reinforces either or both of these destructive postures: The believer is to be a helpless and dependent child and /or an evil creature constantly under the threat of divine rejection.

Acting on the basis of these false selves makes us virtually incapable of intimacy. Any close relationship reawakens the feeling that we must play the role of a helpless, obedient child or a bad person or both as the price of intimacy. We may also believe that revealing our true thoughts and feelings will again precipitate abandonment. We fear that if someone really gets to know us, rejection is sure to follow.

Later in life we may find ourselves being overly accommodating to our teachers, bosses, friends, or lovers. When rejected or hurt, we may blame ourselves. Just as our parents emotionally, if not physically, abandoned us as children, so as adults we abandon our real self and the residual child within us, criticizing ourselves unmercifully or refusing to act on our own behalf. When we identify with these false selves and feel like a helpless child or a bad person, we lose touch with our real self.

In public Jack was the picture of self-confident success. His firm always chose him to negotiate the toughest contracts. In private Jack was passive and obsequious. His wife demanded; he felt he had no choice but to comply. On the phone with an adversary he was forceful and direct. With his wife, his only response was an eagerness to please. His wife was not a particularly demanding person. But his passivity around the house forced her increasingly to take charge of the finances, vacations, and decisions about home repairs. He always acceded to her suggestions. He could not imagine that love did not have to be earned by submission.

These roles that conceal our real self can lead to either a flight from intimacy or a premature settling into a marriage, career, or commitment to an authoritarian religious, political, social, or professional organization that provides a prefabricated identity. The tasks we face as adults—becoming contributing members of society, learning to create and to be productive, and especially forming intimate relationships—depend on a solid sense of who we are. Entering relationships without access to the real self often represents an escape from identity and intimacy rather than an expression of them. Occasionally a person who lacks a strong sense of self gets lucky and in young adulthood enters an intimate relationship that provides a safe and nurturing context in which developmental deficiencies can be repaired. But in my experience such unions are rare when contracted by young people, who are usually unaware of who they are and what they value. More often these unions end in divorce.

Martha's father forgot about her as soon as her brother, Billy, was born. Martha was four at the time. She can still remember her father picking her up and throwing her gently into the air and catching her when he came home from work each night. Her last happy memory of him was the week they were alone together in the house while her mother was in the hospital with Martha's newborn brother. Her father read her a story every night that week. It all ended when little Billy came home. No matter what she did, she could not win back her father's attention. In school she got all A's; Billy got B's and C's. She starred in every school play; Billy did nothing but watch TV after school. Still, when her father came home, Billy was the one he spoke to. On the weekends, Billy was the one who always accompanied him on his errands. And in the spring and summer her father and Billy would go downtown to the ball game, leaving Martha home with her mother, who was always too busy with laundry and vacuuming to talk.

In college Martha met Bryce. His mother's family had been in this country since the Revolutionary War. Bryce's father was an alcoholic. As a boy Bryce would lie in bed at night listening to his parents fight and wish his father would hit him instead of his mother. He'd dream of the day when he'd be big enough to protect her.

That day came when Bryce was a freshman in high school and as tall as his father. During one of their nightly battles, Bryce strolled from his room, walked up to his father, and punched him, knocking him out cold. Instead of being grateful, his mother called the police on Bryce. Family connections kept the case out of court. Bryce was sent to boarding school, where he kept to himself and made few friends. He was too ashamed of himself and his family to let others get to know him. He was afraid they'd ask questions. During vacations Bryce visited his grandmother in Massachusetts.

Martha and Bryce were in an acting class together. For the first few weeks they never spoke to each other. Bryce continued his habit of remaining aloof and staying on the outskirts of the group. He looks so hurt and lonely, Martha thought. She was drawn to him. Without really realizing what she was doing, she plotted her strategy to win him. She started slowly, making small talk about the class. She used all of her considerable acting talents to play exactly the role she thought he'd like. Although he had never acted before, he knew a lot about plays and playwrights from his high school English classes. She discovered it was relatively easy to engage him in conversation about the theater. By the end of the term they were studying together. By the end of the year they were living together in his off-campus apartment. Both stayed at school over the summer, ostensibly to take courses but actually to be together.

She was vivacious and charming; he was attentive and a brilliant conversationalist. Here was a distant man Martha could finally win. Here was a warm, caring woman to take away the pain Bryce felt. They basked in each other's attention. Dates were wonderful. Living together was hell.

After they moved in together, he became jealous and possessive. Every time she returned from class, he'd cross-examine her on whom she had talked to. On her own since childhood, Martha could not stand anyone trying to control her. She fought back by screaming and throwing books at him. Once a month he went to Massachusetts for the weekend to see his grandmother. When he refused to take Martha, she began to scream and throw books at him again, saying she wasn't good enough to meet his family. The screaming reminded him of his childhood, and unable to get her to stop, he walked out and spent the night at a motel. By the end of summer school they had forgotten what had attracted each to the other, and she moved back home till September. Except for occasional glimpses across the campus, they never saw each other again.

The relationship between identity and intimacy is more complex than a simple movement from one to the other. On one hand, identity is a precondition for real intimacy. On the other hand, real selfhood develops only in the context of intimacy (such as between child and parents or other caregivers). Thus weaknesses in identity can be healed only within a relationship or relationships. Empathic interest and realistic feedback were necessary to strengthen the real self in the first place; they are likewise crucial to the recovery of the real self when it has been lost.

Thomas, called Thin Man because he was over six feet and skinny, had carried a gun to junior high school. His older brother, Reg, had been shot the month before his sixteenth birthday in a dispute over drug money. All of Thomas's teachers had said he'd never amount to anything and would end up next to Reg in the cemetery by the Baptist church. At night Thomas fantasized about being a doctor, but his friends were into mugging people downtown. Before he could graduate from high school Thomas was in the state reformatory for juveniles.

Three nights each week a teacher from the local town came to the reformatory to teach any inmates who were interested. At first Thomas attended these classes because there was nothing else to do. But this volunteer teacher took an interest in Thomas and encouraged him. While serving his time Thomas finished his high school degree, and after he was released he attended the local junior college on a special state scholarship. He never became a doctor, but he did become a nurse and worked the emergency room in the city hospital in his old neighborhood.

No one can give what they have not first received. The goal of parental love and intimacy is to prepare the child for adult love and intimacy. If that love was lacking, then the adult's capacity for later love is stunted, and only new love can renew it.

Intimacy is the crucible in which the real self is formed, and real selfhood is a precondition for intimacy. This paradox constitutes the triumph and the tragedy of so many relationships today. A relationship with a parent, child, lover, or spouse must be nurturing and flexible in order to support the process of identity formation or transformation. Yet a minimum sense of self is necessary even to begin such a relationship. This is the conundrum so many face today: The experience of intimacy is necessary to heal the lesions of our spirit, but it is precisely those wounds that keep intimacy at bay.

Ironically it is precisely those who most desperately need nurturing relationships in order to improve their sense of self who can least make such relationships work. They are driven to use every relationship to supply what they feel is missing within themselves. Thus they drain all those they come in contact with. Relationships between two such needy people often feel like two half-empty glasses, each desperately trying to fill themselves from a too-meager supply. They become enraged when they can't get enough of what they need.

Development is an ongoing process in which, ironically, only relationships lead to autonomy. Taking in the environment is the only way to separate from it. In the normal course of development, we gradually take over the functions of our parents. We learn to control our own behavior, to calm ourself, to find our own nurturance. These parental functions become a part of us, and we become independent of our parents. Because we were first cared for, we have learned to care for ourself and are no longer totally dependent on external caregivers. And so we are also in a position to care for others.

A lack of sufficient experiences of parental care, support, encouragement, and advice leaves us psychologically dependent on parents or parent surrogates long after physical independence has been achieved. We cannot incorporate what we have not experienced. If, therefore, we do not internalize caretaking experiences (because we were rarely exposed to them), we will feel intensely dependent on others to supply those missing segments of our selfhood. We will remain dependent on others for feelings of worth, confidence, attractiveness, competency, and so on.

Some of us were forced to separate too quickly into a premature autonomy because adequate supplies of nurturance and support were not available or circumstances forced us to grow up too fast. The result is not independence but a pseudo or defensive autonomy concealing deep dependencies too painful to face. Before we can truly separate, we must first have been truly joined.

Development does not mean that we abandon the relationships from our childhood but only that those relationships become primarily internal rather than external. Leaving home does not mean leaving the family behind but rather living with them primarily inside our head. There the family remains as the template of future involvements. What modern physics has shown to be true of the physical world is also true of the psychological world—even those among us with the strongest sense of self forever remain, both internally and externally, within a field of interaction.

Today many psychologists seem preoccupied with our struggle for independence and the threats posed by the encroachments of others (often primarily the mother). They focus almost exclusively on the acquisition of a virtually isolated and self-sustaining individuality as the hallmark of maturity. They overlook our need to give of ourself. In reality we develop real selfhood out of the bonds of infancy, not only for the sake of autonomous action but also to make possible new forms of relationship. We break free from the womb of symbiosis not in order to fall into atomistic isolation but for the sake of the more profound and complex unions and reunions to come.

The task of the first half of life is to strengthen the real self, not so we can rest content in our isolated identity, but so we can increasingly give that self away to others—to lovers, children, friends, to the wider world of work and culture, and to that which is the source of all. This is a fundamental paradox: We must develop a strong sense of self before we can give that self away; but it is only in giving ourself away that we finally find ourself.

Until we have acquired a vital sense of self, any relationship with another person, a group, or God will threaten to submerge our identity. Such relationships will usually be contaminated by the dynamics of false selfhood and will represent either a regression to the symbiosis of infancy or the brittle power struggles of the rebellious self. Before we can truly join with others, we must first have truly separated.

DISCOVERING OUR true self is a necessary part of mature and satisfying occupational choices and interpersonal commitments. Mary Ann could not become the person she wanted to be until she found and embraced her real self. Only then could she lose weight, decide what she wanted to do with her life, and commit herself to a relationship.

Spiritual development too depends on recovering our core self. Concealed by the facade of false selfhood, the divine image lies in the depths of our inner world. Such a journey of self-discovery may demand great courage as we face the truth about our life and the pain buried there. But without such courage, personal intimacy and spiritual connection may elude us. The recovery of intimacy and spirituality both depend on the process of self-discovery: breaking through these false selves and encountering the real self within. And there is no discovery of that real self except back through the pain and grief associated with its loss.

CHAPTER 4

What Else Can I Do?

THE BMW struck the guardrail twice, flipped over, sailed over the precipice and burst into flames. On his back, thrown free by the impact of auto against earth, Tom watched his car flash across the night sky like an ancient comet burning itself out in a final plunge through space. Then the car disappeared from view and everything went black. He didn't hear the sirens or see the police or remember the careening ambulance ride or feel the surgeons cutting cloth and flesh from his body.

When Tom finally opened his eyes, all was blurry; he could barely make out the cracks winding their way across the hospital ceiling. It took several hours for him to discover that he could not move. Paralyzed! The thought pierced the fog inside his head and froze what little awareness he had. Later in the day, as the blurriness cleared, he gradually realized that he could not tell whether he was actually paralyzed or not, for he was bandaged from head to foot and strapped to a brace.

Days went by before he was fully conscious of his surroundings. Weeks passed before the doctors could say anything definite about his condition, and more weeks elapsed before he could absorb the reality that it would be months before he was up and around again.

For days the only people who appeared were a few nodding and poking doctors and cadres of efficient nurses making their rounds. Yes, they assured him, he could have visitors. But no visitors arrived. He drifted from uncharted, foggy regions of half-consciousness to sharp but fleeting moments of awareness of the room, the tubes, the drab green chairs, and the checkered ceiling. He drank in these seconds of clarity, knowing they would soon succumb to the haze in his brain. Perhaps it's just as well, he thought, in one of these instants of lucidity, that no one's visiting since I hardly seem to be here at all. But the cold loneliness joined the chilling fear of paralysis that was gripping him.

Then one day, as the nurse was rushing out, his ex-wife unexpectedly appeared at the door. In her hand was the little hand of their eight-year-old daughter, Alison, who hesitantly followed her mother into the room. Tom turned his head, the only part of his body that could move, and smiled. He could speak, but there wasn't much to say. Nevertheless they came practically every other day to spend a few hours by his bed. Tom and Janet sat in almost total silence, but Alison was full of questions—none of which he knew the answers to—about the hospital, the machinery, and his condition. She would tell him about school, friends, and the adventures of her dog.

Ah, the dog, he thought. I would never let her have a pet, and now I see how happy that silly mutt makes her. I really love her, he thought, looking at the small, freckled face. But I would never say a thing like that. All of a sudden there seemed a lot to feel regretful about. But it was too late.

As if possessing a will of their own, his thoughts moved to that day, two years ago, when Janet left. Theirs had seemed like the perfect marriage: Tom blazing a golden trail up and down Wall Street; Janet keeping a spotless house, arranging colorful parties, and working part-time as an editor of children's books. Then, one spring day, as a warm breeze drifted across Central Park and into their apartment, she announced that they had grown too distant and never talked. It's true, Tom thought, there's nothing I can say in refutation, we don't ever talk anymore. And so, she had said, I'm moving. He remembered protesting halfheartedly, hardly conscious of what was happening. Odd, he thought, looking back from the perspective of two years, neither of us said anything about trying again or working on it. We just let eight years of our lives go without even a fight.

Janet was gone less than a month when Tom got involved with a young analyst in his firm. He recalled warmly her adoration, her appreciation of his brilliance, and her interest in his work. So unlike Janet, with her prim efficiency. They lasted almost a year. Then she started talking about wanting more, and he, smelling marriage again, disappeared from her life without a call.

Even without the anesthetic haze in his brain, the last year was a blur. Lying in bed, he could hardly bring it into focus: a roller coaster of two- or three-week flings, lots of expensive dinners, shows, weekend trips—make a big impression, then flee. He could barely remember some of the women. No wonder none of them come to visit me, he thought.

Almost two months to the day from his admittance, the doctors put him under again and cut him loose from his sarcophagus of bandages. He went into the anesthesia with fear and anticipation, knowing that when he awoke he would discover if he'd ever be able to walk or jog or drive or make love again. The doctors were not sure about the extent of his injuries. The CAT scan showed nothing permanent, but they said they wouldn't know for sure until he was unbandaged and free to move.

He opened his eyes to sunlight burning through the window and felt a blessed tingling in his arms and legs. For the first time in his adult life, Tom found tears in his eyes. He pushed himself through a daily regimen of physical therapy. Three weeks later he was walking the length of the hospital hall, balancing on two canes.

The day he was to be discharged, a sheriff appeared with the doctor. "We did blood tests when you first got here," the white-coated figure explained, "and we found cocaine in your blood."

Tom wasn't sure what to think. "Right from the hospital to the jail?" he asked sardonically. "At least the food won't be worse than the stuff here." His Wall Street–bred gallows humor had not deserted him.

"No," the sheriff said, almost smiling at Tom's self-mockery, "but you will have to appear in court next month to answer charges of driving while under the influence of drugs."

"Perhaps I could throw myself on the mercy of the court," Tom wondered out loud to his firm's attorney. A month hence he would still have bandages around his forehead, chest, and legs and would require a wheelchair for any distance. "Perhaps," the lawyer said, and Tom remembered he was a man of few words.

Words were not necessary. Apparently the judge felt pity looking down from the bench on the bandaged figure rolling before him in a wheelchair. Tom was given a steep fine and two years' probation with mandatory drug testing, and he lost his license for only a year. The lawyer had been brief but eloquent about how Tom had learned his lesson.

"What lesson have I learned?" Tom asked me the first time we met.

"I feel like a concept," he told me. "I am an abstraction, and it's hard to get to know an abstraction. When I'm at work—phones ringing, computer screens flashing, millions of dollars resting on a split-second decision (or so I tell myself)—I can almost hear the crowds on the street cheering each brilliant move. It's a real high, like a gambler with dice in his hands. I feel plugged in, energized. Other than that, I am just an idea going through life in a three-piece suit."

Throughout his life Tom had been exquisitely sensitive to the opinions of others. All those months of lying in the hospital had forced him to turn inward, to try to draw on his own inner resources. But he found there only a void. With no cheering or criticizing voices around him, he had no inner gyroscope to guide him. All his sensors pointed outside and none inside. Isolated in the antisepsis of the hospital room, he floundered emotionally and grew more and more depressed as he sank into that inner emptiness.

Nothing to do meant nothing to live for. Or, he had started to think, nothing to do meant no place to run from having nothing to live for.

He'd never thought much about his life and had tried to push the questions away. Yet in the loneliness of the hospital room, with nothing to do but think, the questions had kept intruding.

"What does my life add up to now?" he had wondered. "The ledger is blank. No co-workers slapping me on the back. No women toasting me over dinner. No walking down Fifth Avenue and buying expensive toys on a whim. What's left?"

That depression had driven him to me after his release.

In response to even the simplest questions about how he was feeling or the experience of the accident, Tom drew a blank. Looking inside, he saw nothing. He was so disconnected from his emotions that any discussion of his feelings was pure conjecture. Blocked, he hit a wall every time he tried to look inward. Listening to him flounder was like listening to a tone-deaf person struggle to talk about a symphony.

At first he tried to guess at an answer to the question about his own feelings and experiences, but what he said was stilted and intellectual and rang hollow in his own ears as well as mine. No wonder Tom's original complaints were rather vague: "I feel a void in my life" was all he could say.

Unwilling to give up on him or let him off the hook, I told him, "Concentrate on that void. If you painted a picture of it, what would it look like? What color would it be? Would it be a moving picture or a still life? If you gave it a voice, what would it say? What tone would it use? Whose voice is it? Male or female?"

Tom tried hard but nothing came. A thousand random thoughts raced through his mind or the inner screen went blank.

"Imagery has never been my thing," he said. "I can't form images in my mind."

"Close your eyes and picture a light bulb," I told him.

At first the outlines were fuzzy but he reported seeing a spot of light in the middle of the blank space in his mind.

"It's OK if it's fuzzy," I reassured him. "It can be on, off, bright, or dim—just picture it there."

After several minutes, the image of the bulb got sharper.

"Now," I urged him, "try turning it on or off and making it lighter or darker."

All he could manage was envisioning a spot of light.

I sent Tom home with the assignment to practice that exercise.

Over the next few days he learned to turn the bulb in his mind on and off and to make it brighter or dimmer. He found he could make it so bright that it flooded his whole field of consciousness.

Having improved his skill at imagery with the light bulb exercise, I suggested another to Tom: "Imagine yourself entering a dark movie theater. No one else is there. Picture yourself taking a comfortable seat where you can see the blank screen. Take some time and really put yourself in that movie house and focus on the screen. Now, just allow any image to come on the screen, any image at all. See it playing there on the screen like a moving picture. Let it run its course and then fade away."

Tom tried to picture a scene from his childhood that he barely remembered.

"No," I told him, "don't try. The trick of this exercise is not to consciously program your movie but simply to allow the images to appear on their own."

But again Tom tensed his forehead and tried to tune in a little boy on a tricycle.

"It won't work that way," I told him again. "The point is to practice letting things come spontaneously."

Such an approach was contrary to Tom's entire style of life. "I need to do, to be active, to make things happen."

"How does it feel not to be able to make things happen," I asked him, "like when you were unable to work, confined to the hospital?"

"That's the void I feel, just empty inside."

"Now, relax, settle into that void. Paint a picture of it. What does it look like?"

"Black, all black. Not the color black. Not anything." Tom felt uncontrollably agitated. He opened his eyes and looked around.

"What do you feel?" I asked.

"Scared. As scared as I've ever felt in my life."

"Can you stick with it?"

"I'm not sure," he answered. He proceeded to miss his next two appointments. When he came back, I saw no reason to make an issue of it other than to point out that he was fleeing.

"I feel caught between a rock and a hard place," Tom said. "Often I feel I can't go through with this. I'm afraid of what I'm going to find inside. I'm afraid maybe there's some dark secret I'm not aware of. Actually I'm most afraid that there is nothing inside me at all."

"Do you want to stop?"

"No. I can't go back to feeling good a couple of minutes each day and empty all the rest of the time."

"Again, what is the emptiness? Picture yourself going into a theater. What appears on the blank screen?"

"Nothing. It's a TV screen, and it's all blank." Tom strained to see something, then remembered my instructions to relax and just watch.

Gradually an image came on the screen. It was Tom as a little boy, riding a tricycle, the same image he had earlier tried so hard to conjure up by willpower. The boy was riding alone, all alone. Down the street he pedaled, slowly and deliberately. But no one else was there. There was no background, no surface, just a preschool boy on a tricycle. Slowly the picture faded from Tom's consciousness, but the memory of it remained.

Tom felt very subdued, almost peaceful.

"How did the boy feel?" I asked.

Tom opened his mouth and started to talk but no words came out. He felt his throat tighten. Tighter and tighter, until he could hardly breathe. Now his stomach was tightening too, gripped by some nameless emotion.

"Lonely," he croaked.

Then the emotion rose from his stomach. His whole chest and throat tightened, and his temples pounded. He left the session early and hobbled as quickly as possible to his car. He raced back to his apartment, holding back his tears. Once inside, the pain of that loneliness burst out in a flood.

"What's happening to me?" Tom cried out into his empty apartment as he staggered from room to room. The image of the boy on the tricycle would not leave his mind. Every time he thought of it, his body convulsed with sobs. He wrapped his arms around his stomach and rocked back and forth, as if trying to comfort himself, but no comfort came. Nothing held back the sobs.

"When have I felt this way before?" he asked himself.

The word *always* echoed in his mind.

"No!" he screamed inwardly. "It can't be. How could I have lived this long with such pain?"

A picture of himself dashing to his desk to make a crucial call to the stock market flashed through his mind.

Work!

"Work has been my salvation," he thought. "Keep busy, keep moving, keep the mind and body running. No time to think. No time to feel. Take out that anger on the competitors or, when deals go bad, on myself. Fill that void with hours on the job, stuff it with dollar bills, buy it off with a new motorcycle or a stereo."

More tears. Fortunately it was Friday night. No dates this weekend. "Who wants to go out with a man who still walks with a cane and has bandages around his ribs and legs?" he wondered sardonically to himself. "Maybe this is the time I should start drinking?"

Never a heavy drinker, Tom poured himself a glass of whiskey and then in anger threw the bottle into the trash. It was still open, and the booze gurgled out into the basket, making the room smell like an old bus terminal.

"No!" he screamed at the draining bottle. "I have drugged myself all my life. I've got to find out what's happening to me."

"It was like a giant open wound inside me," Tom told me later. "It drained and filled and drained again and again and again."

He slept fitfully that night. The next day, Saturday, he settled himself by watching movies on cable TV and at night fell into an exhausted sleep.

At two in the morning he found himself awake, sweating and shaking, fragments of a dream trying to rearrange themselves in his mind. There was some futuristic battle with laser-beam weapons and red-and-yellow bombs. Then he was escaping, riding on horseback in a cowboy outfit. Then he was in his boat in a storm; the boat capsized, and he was thrown into the turbulent ocean. There must be sharks, he remembered thinking. Then, sure enough, a fin appeared in the water, and a huge set of teeth rushing at him like a scene from *Jaws*. In the dream he screamed and closed his eyes, and the next thing he knew he was floating on his back in a calm sea.

Shaken, he put on the light, went to the kitchen, and poured himself a glass of milk. For a long time he just stared out the window, not even seeing the gleaming lights of the city. Unknown minutes later, he went back to sleep.

It was Sunday noon when he awoke, sunlight filling the room. He felt weak but calm. It was as if a fever had broken, and now he was free of it. He took a walk outside and thought the city never looked brighter or more vibrant.

On Monday he was still weak, and his eyes remained swollen from all the tears.

"Hard weekend, Tom?" one of his co-workers sneered, cynically wondering what kind of wild weekend a man with a cane and a bandaged groin could have.

Tom ignored him and slid into his chair. Orders were piled up on his desk along with sheets and sheets of neatly folded computer paper, filled with numbers. Last week he couldn't wait to see the latest figures; now the numbers blurred before his eyes. He put the papers down, turned his chair, and looked out the window. All he could see were the rows of windows in the building next door, but he gazed outside anyway.

"It seems a waste of my life," he found himself thinking, "just being a high-stakes gambler with other people's money. But what else can I do?"

"What else can I do?" That question haunted him as he sat alone at lunch. It came home with him on the bus ride uptown. It stayed with him all through the night.

Sitting at work the next day he remembered reading about a service that used experienced businessmen as consultants for minority businesses that could not afford financial advisers. He dug the article out of the paper and soon began to volunteer his time.

After leaving Tom, Janet had moved north of the city. The rows of neighboring townhouses contained a horde of children Alison's age. There Alison could make friends and walk safely to a nearby elementary school. At first Tom rarely saw her. He was supposed to take her every Sunday and a weekend a month, but more often than not he called with an excuse. At first Janet argued with him and demanded he visit because she saw the disappointment on Alison's face each Sunday. But after a year of getting nowhere with Tom, Janet learned not to count on him.

After his hospital stay, Tom found himself frequently thinking about Alison. The end of their regular meetings by his bedside, strained and silent as they often were, evoked a gnawing sadness in him. He found himself wondering what she was doing. And he had little to do in his spare time. He wanted to see her again.

Unable to drive or walk very far, he called Janet and asked if she would bring Alison into the city or put her on the train. Gradually they worked out a schedule: Janet would spend Sundays in the city, dropping Alison off at Tom's apartment in the morning and picking her up in the evening.

With the divorce they had sold their Central Park cooperative, and Tom had moved into a one-bedroom apartment closer to work. Not much room there for a little girl to play. But there was a city park down the block that even Tom could walk to, and on nice days they went there. Later Alison stayed over one Saturday each month, sleeping in Tom's room while he used the living room couch. As his time with Alison increased, Tom moved to a two-bedroom townhouse so she could have her own room when she stayed with him.

Tom was surprised at how much he enjoyed these times. His own parents, proprietors of a tool and die business, had approached parenthood with the same efficiency and determination they brought to their business. Actually the business had consumed many of their evenings and weekends. Tom had few good memories of times with his parents. Not knowing how to be a parent, he had found it easier to avoid spending time with Alison. But it was becoming natural to hold her hand, to go to the movies, to push her on the swings, to eat ice cream with her. And words bubbled out of her if he just listened.

After several months of volunteer consulting and spending more time with his daughter, Tom felt pretty good about himself.

"For the first time I'm reaching out to others," he said to me one day, "seeing what I can give rather than what I can get. That makes me feel better about myself." Also the last of the bandages had come off, and the cane spent most of the day in the closet. Tom was a free man. Feeling satisfied with his life, Tom stopped therapy.

A year later, walking home from a consulting job, he felt the old void opening up inside again. No, he protested inwardly, I thought you were gone for good—addressing the void as if it were another person. But it was back. Gradually the return of the void forced him to face the reality that he was getting bored with his brand of financial social work. Helping others was supposed to fill the void, but it didn't. The feeling that something was still missing nipped at the edges of his mind. True, he thought, I have still not settled into a relationship; but is that the goal of life? No, he answered his own question, I've been in many relationships, more than I can count, and none filled this void. I'm not depressed, he reassured himself. But the idea of "taking the next step" reverberated in his mind. So he called me.

"Next step where?" I asked when he came to my office the following day.

"I don't know, that's why I'm here."

We discussed his question, but the conversation didn't seem to get anywhere.

That night he dreamed of a young boy on a tricycle riding alone across a desert.

"When you imagine a desert, what do you think of?" I asked him later.

The first thing that popped into Tom's mind was the word *emptiness*. He saw an image of a vast expanse of sand, stretching onward and onward, with no living thing. Dead. Barren.

Tom suddenly felt sick to his stomach.

"That's my worst fear. Nothing there. That I am a hollow man after all. An empty tube filled with hot air."

The bottom seemed to drop right out of his stomach and open onto a vast endless space.

Several nights later Tom had one of the worst nightmares of his life. There was Wall Street at noon bustling with impeccably dressed, briefcase-toting men and women rushing past each other to important meetings. Then, suddenly, the whole scene turned into a heap of sand dunes. All the people vanished and there were only waves of sand, the endless desert. He awoke gripped by panic, unable to fall asleep again no matter how much he tried to relax. And it was no comfort to go to work the next morning and find the buildings and the people still intact, for he was unable to drive from his mind the image of Wall Street becoming a pile of sand.

Unable to concentrate on his work, he called me from his office. I had an opening at 4:30 that afternoon. Tom was there at 3:45.

Once in my office, he was relieved to sink into the familiar brown easy chair. Automatically Tom found himself breathing more deeply, attending to the tingling and stretching sensations of relaxation, and settling into a calmer state. The desert image again appeared in his mind.

"It's true," he said in my office, reflecting on his dream, "my work covered the void I felt. I was like an actor playing a role, but the audience of clients and onlookers was responding to the role, not to me. No wonder I never felt much satisfaction from those few moments of excitement. It wasn't simply that they didn't last. Even while they were happening, it wasn't really me that was being appreciated, only the part I was playing. And there really wasn't much of me there to appreciate. Behind the three-piece suit was only a cipher.

"And my consulting for charity," he continued in this unusually self-reflective mode, "that too expressed another self—a self seeking some meaning. I was still looking for it in activities, in the responses of others. I felt good as long as I was appreciated by my poor, underprivileged clients. There's nothing wrong with those things, with trading or with consulting, but they don't fill the void."

A few days later Tom found himself driving toward the shore and decided to check on his boat. He had bought it years ago, another toy with which to amuse himself and impress his friends. It had sat in storage for more than a year now. His only contact with it had been paying the storage fees and promising himself that he would sell it, but he hadn't gotten around to it. He was surprised to find it clean, polished, and ready to go. The dock owner had taken good care of it. Well, at least my money has gone for something, he thought.

"Want to take it out?" the dock man asked. "I can have it tuned up and in the water for you in a couple hours."

"Why not?" Tom found himself saying. "One last ride before I put it up for sale."

He walked around the waterfront town, had a bite of lunch, and two hours later was pulling out of the slip. When he returned at sunset, instead of asking the dock man for a "For Sale" sign, he rented a slip for the summer, even though he wasn't sure why.

In good weather he and Alison would go fishing together. She seemed to enjoy sitting in the boat with her line in the water. On those rare occasions when either of them would hook a fish, she laughed with excitement. He was glad to see her so happy.

At least one afternoon each weekend, he tried to take the boat out into the ocean by himself. Instead of racing and jumping waves, he would shut the motor off and just drift, engulfed in the silence of sea and air. He let himself settle down into the silence, punctuated only by occasional waves or seagulls. Over the months that stillness grew more constant within him. Alone. But isn't it odd, he thought later, I don't feel lonely out here at all. Instead his mind seemed to expand in the expanse of the sea until it touched or was touched by everything around him—the water, the clouds, the blue sky.

The following Monday, swept along the sidewalk by the hordes of suits and briefcases, the same sensation of connection to his surroundings, including the harsh pavement and the impenetrable towers, was evoked within him.

And the tiny yard behind his townhouse began to call out for a garden. Not much of one in a space only fifteen by twenty feet or so. He and Alison put in a few tomato plants, some flowers, and a couple of rose bushes in the part that got regular sun.

One morning Tom found a memo on his desk asking if anyone wanted to write in their field of expertise for a newsletter the firm was starting. Tom stared at that memo for a long time. It's time to take a little risk, something inside of him said. No, he protested, this is my private thing. But the inner prompting grew stronger. Weary of fighting it, Tom succumbed and wrote a memo back stating that he didn't want to say anything more about stocks and bonds but was willing to try writing something "a little more personal."

"What does that mean?" his boss asked.

"I'm not sure," Tom confessed. "Let me just try and see what happens."

That sounded risk-free, and Tom started submitting columns not only about quarterly reports and computer services but also about loneliness in the midst of a crowded office and the jumble of feelings that occur when one comes to work and finds an empty and clean desk where yesterday there was a co-worker and everybody knows he's been fired but nobody says anything. Ideas for columns would pop into his head while he was drifting with the waves or pruning his roses.

"Am I losing my mind?" he asked me one day.

"Do you feel you're losing your mind? Do you feel out of touch with reality?" I asked.

No, Tom had to admit. He actually felt better and seemed to be able to read more clearly what people were saying to him. He was struck with how often in the past he had listened merely to the words people used and had responded to those. Now he was aware of other aspects. He could sometimes sense when someone was holding something back or when they weren't completely convinced of what they were saying. He listened more and talked less, often asking his clients and associates, "Is that all?" or "Isn't there something more?" or "Do you really think that's true?" He felt like he was guessing less, even though he was relying on his intuition more.

No, he thought to himself, looking back over the previous months, I do feel more in touch with reality, not less.

One day, saying he was feeling stronger and calmer, Tom asked about ending therapy. I asked him to think about what had been the most important changes in his life.

"In the past," he said, "I felt like an outsider, playing a game but standing aloof from it. Now I feel a part of what I do. I'm more open with the people I work with. The column helps a lot. People don't always know how to respond, but I'm respected enough that I can get away with it. And writing that little column helps me feel that there's more of me in my work.

"And the outdoors," he continued. "Being out in nature has really changed me. Made me aware of how isolated I was. Cut off. From myself. I never thought of myself as creative. My work was purely technical. I was just like a computer—input the data and output the decision of when to buy and when to sell. It's a lot more complicated than that; I'm a lot more complicated than that.

"Now I know what the word *recreation* really means—re-creation. The boat really is a re-creational device; I re-create myself every time I go out there and let myself just go with the currents of the sea. But it's not just the water and the waves. Through them I've begin to sense a 'presence.' That's the only word I can use.

"I picked up a book I read in college years ago. Actually I didn't really read it back then. It was assigned, and I read a few pages and then put in down in disgust. It's called *I and Thou*, by Martin Buber, and just the other day I came across a passage where he writes, 'We receive, and what we receive is not a "content" but a presence, a presence as strength.' That really captures my experience. Drifting alone out in the ocean has given me a sense of presence, that someone, something, is there with me. And Buber goes on to call this . . . here, I wrote it down." Tom took a piece of paper from his shirt pocket and continued, "Buber calls this experience of presence 'the inexpressible confirmation of meaning. Nothing can henceforth be meaningless.' Buber says, 'The question of the meaning of life has vanished. We do not know how to pinpoint or define the meaning, we lack any image or formula for it, yet it is more certain than the sensations of the senses.'" Tom folded the paper and put it back in his pocket and continued, "I'm not sure I'm really putting it into words, but I'm aware that something's there—a presence inside me and outside—that I never knew about before. I've never been a religious person, but recently I've started to wonder: Is that what other people call God?"

CHAPTER 5

The Malaise of Modernity

What we fear above all, and what keeps the new world powerless to be born, is that if we give up our dream of private success for a more genuinely integrated societal community, we will be abandoning our separation and individuation, collapsing into dependency and tyranny. ROBERT BELLAH, ET AL., *Habits of the Heart*

To PROTECT ourself against the pain we have learned to associate with intimacy, we avoid closeness with others and with God. Such connections often remain elusive because they touch our deepest fear and anxiety—born of our false selves—that relationships with others and with a universal and cosmic presence lead to the loss of the individuality and autonomy that we prize so much. These forces within us interfere with our desire for relationships. But there are also factors within our society that make such connections difficult.

It is no coincidence that fears of intimacy seem widespread in our culture. In their study of American attitudes toward culture and community entitled *Habits of the Heart*, Robert Bellah and his associates describe the collapse of community in America, chronicling in the wider culture the social side of what psychotherapists see in the privacy of their consulting rooms. Their thesis could well be summed up in the paragraph that opens this chapter: Fear of "collapsing into dependency and tyranny" keeps us isolated, clinging to our fragile feeling of autonomy.

The historical background to our dread of dependency lies in the transition from the Middle Ages to modern society.

Medieval culture was basically organic. Identity came from belonging—belonging to a hierarchical society in which everything fit together and had a place and therefore a purpose, belonging to the one and only church, belonging to a sacred cosmos presided over by a providential and paternalistic God.

With the coming of the forces of modern culture (which I will simply call *modernity*), the collective structures of Christendom fragmented into warring nationalities, sects, economic classes. Italian, German, and French cultures become conscious of their separate national identities apart from Christendom. The rise of trade created new economic groups not dependent on the feudal order. The new learning of the Renaissance generated a kaleidoscope of intellectual paradigms beyond those of late medieval theology. The Reformation brought on by Luther, Calvin, and others introduced pluralism into the field of religion. Eventually these collectivities of nation, sect, and class further atomized into autonomous but isolated individuals. The sense of belonging was replaced by an emphasis on the individual. Modernity liberated the individual from the shackles of church and state and family and class and opened the way to the pursuit of private interests.

Freed from ties to the past by the criticism of tradition and from each other by the fragmentation of society, the individual has little protection from rootlessness and isolation. Such liberation brings separation from human community. Thus the major psychological problem of modernity becomes, as all of us (psychotherapists or not) know, preserving that isolated and fragile sense of selfhood in the face of the vast, impersonal natural and social forces that surround us. Contemporary plays, novels, and psychotherapeutic literature depict unleashed impulses, shattered relationships, withdrawn people—the interior side of the social forces that shape modern culture.

ONE OF the major carriers of modernity was natural science, which dismantled the sacred cosmos of premodern sensibility and re-created the world as a vast system of levers and pulleys. After Newton, everywhere men went, they listened for (and therefore heard) nothing but the hum of machinery. Modernity's goal was to transform the world into a technological problem. One by one the tasks of governing the state, healing the sick, guiding the economy, choosing right and wrong, and understanding human nature became "sciences"—that is, governed by measurement and the desire for control.

The metaphor of the machine began to dominate Western images of the cosmos, lower organisms, and even human life at precisely the time that gargantuan steam engines began to dominate the landscape of Europe and America.

Now we are inclined to see even ourselves as merely genes or complicated chemical reactions. Whereas the psalmist says that *Homo sapiens* is only slightly lower than angels, I recently heard an expert in artificial intelligence say that we are only computers made of flesh. Describing everything in mechanical terms undermines our capacity for experiencing wonder, awe, reverence, spontaneity, and mystery in relationship to nature, other people, and even in relationship to ourself.

The medieval sensibility saw the worlds of nature, politics, religion, and economics as simply given—established by divine fiat and grounded in God's natural law. The contours of the physical world, the structures of the church, the doctrines of theology, the organization of the state were fixed and unchanging—reflections of an ideal, heavenly world. Individuals could only submit themselves to the divine order, resigned to their place in the social and economic hierarchy, surrendering to the mystery of divine sovereignty.

The experience of the world as fixed and the imperative of submission to a higher power are central in all religious traditions, for all the major religions arose before the advent of modernity. But what will become of religion now that this crucial image of submission to a higher or greater reality is losing credibility?

Science shattered that sensibility. It is impossible for us to recapture the excitement that bubbles through the writings of men like Kepler, Newton, and Galileo and that gripped the minds of men and women in the sixteenth and seventeenth centuries as word spread that the human mind could grasp the central order of nature and transcribe the celestial spheres into terrestrial mathematics.

Along with science came technology. The physical world could not only be understood, it could be changed. No longer prisoners of an unchanging and unchangeable natural order, we have become masters of our destiny. If we don't like the way the river runs, we plow it up. If we don't like the way our society functions, it is our duty (as the Declaration of Independence says) to alter it. We can choose when and how many children to have; soon we will be able to choose their sex, talents, and physical attributes. We live less and less in the immediate world of nature and more and more in a world shaped exclusively by our own hands.

We view the natural and social worlds as infinitely plastic in our technological hands. We also see the world as the playground of randomness and chance. Our best scientific theories assume that the universe burst into being from the chance collision of a few primal particles, and the living world of blooming orchids, singing robins, and cogitating scientists sprang from the random mating of macromolecules. The point is not to dispute these theories but only to suggest ways in which they, like Newtonian science and technological reason, have changed our vision of the world and ourselves.

Though we are taught that everything around us is the product of randomness, we know ourselves to be agents of purpose. We plan, predict, and control. Therefore why should we subject ourselves to blind chance? We have not only the possibility of shaping nature to suit our purposes, we have the duty to do so. As agents of reason we must impose rational order on reasonless chaos.

I was once teaching a class on ethics and was sent a book on genetic engineering entitled *From Chance to Purpose*—a title that said it all. Through the technological imperative we free ourselves from the tyranny of chance and bring predictability into our lives. For example, the gender, intelligence, and abilities of our children are the result of pure genetic roulette but, for the next generation of parents, through surgical-chemical intervention, these will be under our control.

So the obsession of the modern age becomes control, and technology has given us the means to act out that obsession. We assume that we must control everything: the weather, our moods, the course of the economy, the production of children. Clinically, one of the major symptoms of our age seems to be the fear of losing control. Many an ulcer, hypertensive state, or anxiety attack begins when contemporary men and women sense their lives slipping out of their control. In my work, time and time again I find that the fear of losing control is at the root of many modern maladies: sexual dysfunction, hesitancy about intimacy, conflicts about having and raising children, and a closed-mindedness about spiritual experience.

Occasionally the need to be in control gets out of control.

Teri came from the most chaotic of families. Both parents were alcoholic. Mother would play straight for a while, and father would remain in a stupor. Then they would change roles: Father would shop and cook, and mother would pass out in bed and not be seen for days. Most often they would get drunk together—their main form of intimacy—and Teri would hide in her room, under the bed, afraid of what they might do to her. There was no reason to fear. They had long since forgotten about her and her older brother sleeping in the next room.

Her brother quit high school and disappeared into the navy. As soon as she graduated, Teri followed him into the military by joining the Women's Air Corps. Six months of barracks and mess halls and the routine of the typing pool and Teri began to blossom like a neglected plant suddenly transplanted to a well-maintained, fenced-in garden. What others found boring and tedious felt like safety to her. Teri signed on for a ten-year hitch.

Freed from the desperate need simply to survive, she went to college with help from the air force, finished with a degree in aeronautical engineering, and obtained her pilot's license along the way. When her air force tour was over, she became one of the first women commercial pilots. She earned the wings of a captain in record time.

Known as the "Ice Maiden" among the other pilots, she was cold, calculating, and always calm under pressure. The walls of her living room soon filled with citations for outstanding professionalism. Respecting her as a colleague, even the most macho of pilots left her alone socially. The rumor was that it was colder crashing in Teri's bed than on the North Pole. That was just a rumor. In fact the one place she would release her iron grip on herself was in bed. There she let go with a reckless fury.

Many men became caught in the excruciating contrast between her steely exterior and her flamboyant sexuality. As soon as any of them showed too much interest in her or became too regular a visitor to her penthouse, she would pick fights, schedule lengthy trips, or rent a private plane and disappear. Neither the warm and caring nor the tough and combative were able to break down the walls she had erected around herself.

One clear night she rented a small plane, circled alone high above the western desert, and, as the first rays of sun glimmered over the rim of the earth, dove the plane into the ground. Federal investigators listed it as an accident, but those who knew her knew otherwise.

Our obsessive drive for control often invades family life as well. The realm of child rearing cannot forever remain a sanctuary protected from the attitudes that beat at us from the media, leap out of our textbooks, govern our commerce, and shape our view of the world. Frequently I see families whose fundamental concern in coming to a therapist is not improving communication or knowing their children better but only finding ways of ensuring that the kids will turn out as expected, just like the latest product off the assembly line.

Psychologically there appears to be a connection between the cultural values of control and detachment and the fear of emotion. Feelings exist outside the perimeters of reason. Because they threaten to break down our carefully wrought walls of control, feelings appear dangerous, chaotic, or threatening. Often their existence is simply denied. Parents frequently come to therapists not to understand but to control, not to learn to be more nurturing but to learn to be more efficient, not to invest more emotion in their children but to keep a tighter lid on what few emotions are there.

How often I have seen parents who seem oblivious to whole realms of life. Of course I'm a good parent, they say. I provide a nice house, new toys, stimulating vacations, a good education, and, sometimes, expensive therapists. They are not (usually) bad or malevolent people; they speak in all sincerity and perplexity, occasionally laced by an anger bred of incomprehension. Vainly do their children (and/or spouse) try to convey to them their appreciation for that bounty and their sense that something crucial is still missing.

Missing are the most important psychological ingredients in the parent-child interaction: empathy, understanding, an emotional investment in the child, and the capacity to take children on their own terms rather than seeing them as extensions of parental images of the good child, the successful student, the popular achiever, and so on. Modernity's values of control, detachment, and efficiency run directly counter to the child's need for empathy and understanding; its flight from feelings runs directly counter to the child's need for nurturance. Without it the child quickly develops a false self—the pleaser who tries vainly to adapt to every parental whim or the rebel who sees every parental action as a move to control or destroy.

Some years ago a series of experiments were conducted by H. F. Harlow in which baby monkeys were caged with surrogate "mothers" made from cloth-covered wire frames. Although adequately fed and sheltered, the lack of interaction caused these monkeys to exhibit emotionally disturbed behavior. These ill-fated monkeys have always struck me as living parables of so much of life in the modern world.

A more profoundly sad example of the same phenomena involves institutionalized infants who were given more than adequate nourishment and shelter but less than adequate human interaction and ended up severely withdrawn and depressed, if not dead. It is a further parable of life in the modern world that one must cite studies like these and devise exercises like the one described earlier, in which my students tried to construct a society on the mechanistic premises of modern culture, in order to try to convince the present age of what should be immediately obvious—that human beings need human connection and not just physical security or impersonal intellectual stimulation in order to thrive.

People raised under the sole dominion of rationalism and efficiency, like Harlow's experimental monkeys bound to wire mother surrogates, find it psychologically impossible to connect with and invest themselves in others, since one cannot give to another what has not first been given to oneself. Those whose real self was never elicited or appreciated cannot mobilize that sense of selfhood when making choices about relationships, vocations, or values. Without that sense of self, intimacy and connection elude us.

There's an anonymous proverb that says, "There are two kinds of insanity: the insanity that comes from losing your reason and the insanity that comes from losing everything but your reason." Modern culture finds itself in precisely the predicament of having lost everything *except* reason.

Lewis Perry, Jr., age fifteen, sat across the office from me, a pile of arms and legs cramped uncomfortably into one of my chairs.

"Do you know why you're here?" I asked for openers.

"My mother said I had to come" was his reply.

Lewis's mother was in therapy with a friend of mine because she was not sure she wanted to remain married to Lewis's father. In the course of their work, it came out that she was concerned about Lewis and that his school had recommended therapy because of a poor social adjustment. My friend referred them to me.

"Why did she say that?" I asked.

"I don't know."

"Do you like school?"

"It's OK."

Lewis sat with his head down, staring at the floor. At first he looked depressed, but the more he talked, the less depressed he seemed and the more uneasy I felt.

"What's your least favorite class?"

"Gym."

"Why don't you like it?"

"I'm flunking it" was his surprising answer.

"How do you flunk gym?" I asked, without concealing my amazement.

"By missing over half the classes," he answered matter-of-factly.

"Why have you done that?"

"Because I don't like it, and so I don't go."

"You just don't go?"

"I tell my mother I'm sick, and she writes a note to excuse me, or on my computer I print out a facsimile of my doctor's stationery with a letter excusing me."

He delivered this in a flat, expressionless tone, and I had to remind myself that I was talking to a high school sophomore.

"How do you feel about lying like that?"

"I don't like gym, I think it's stupid, I'm not going to play on a team, I don't want to be a jock, and I don't think I should have to do something that's stupid."

"But what will happen if you flunk?"

"That's their problem, not mine; I'm an honors student, and they're not going to keep an honors student, who will surely be going to one of the best universities, from graduating because of gym."

"Do you have friends?" I asked later.

"Yes, two."

"Tell me about them."

"Tom and Jonathan, we're all in the computer club at school."

"How often do you see them outside of school?"

"Almost every day, they come over to my house and we work on our computers; my family has several, and so we can all do our projects at the same time."

"Do you work together on them?"

"Not really, we each work at our own set; sometimes we'll discuss what we're doing, but we're all pretty independent thinkers."

As he spoke about this work, the vaguest ray of feeling lightened his face momentarily, but then it lapsed back into flatness. His time with his friends sounded more like the parallel play of preschoolers than the give-and-take of young adult friendships.

The more Lewis talked, the more worried about him I became. I didn't feel I was making contact with the person inside him. It was as if he had sent his jeans and shirt and glasses but had refused to come himself. Several times I wanted to shake him and say, Lewis, are you in there? But I refrained. Gradually the interview wound down, and Lewis simply refused to talk anymore, saying, "I don't think I should be here. I don't have any problems."

I talked to his parents. "Doctor Perry," as he introduced himself, was a large, hulking man who worked as a chemical engineer. Apparently he had agreed to come only once to see me in order to meet the person who might be working with his son. Mrs. Perry was a little plump, neatly dressed, and inclined to smile all the time.

"Well, Doctor," Lewis's father began, "what did you think of our son?"

"Why don't you tell me first what you think the problem is?"

"Afraid to commit yourself, eh? OK, I don't think there's any problem with our family; there's no reason for us to be here."

"But," I said, "your wife is in treatment, and the school has asked you to get treatment for Lewis. Something must be going on."

"My wife is just going through her change of life. Our son will soon be leaving home, and she's having trouble deciding what she wants to do next. As for the school, they're all upset because he's not going out with girls—they push kids too fast socially at that school. He's getting all A's, his science project came in second in the state; tell me, Doctor, where's the problem?"

Mrs. Perry did nothing to contradict her husband's minimization of her concerns, and so I asked if she agreed.

"Of course," she said sweetly, "all that school is concerned about is socializing, but any girl who would date boys at this age is probably no good."

"Does Lewis have friends?" I asked, and they went on at great length about the two boys from the computer club but could not describe anything the boys did as a group or anything much they did as a family.

"Now that the boy has grown up," Dr. Perry said, "we're all pretty independent."

"Do you have any problems with Lewis at home?" I asked.

There was a moment of stunned silence, like I had stumbled onto a great secret.

"Well, now that you mention it," Dr. Perry said, "he is pretty disobedient at home."

"How?"

"He never does his chores."

"What chores?"

"The garbage, cleaning his room, and cutting the lawn. He just never seems to do them, and we have to remind him constantly."

"What do you do when he doesn't do them?"

"Punish him."

"How?"

"Oh, I suppose you're one of those psychologists who doesn't believe in punishment, eh?"

I reassured him that I was not one of "those" psychologists, but I did want to know about Lewis's life.

"Well, frankly, nothing has worked—we're thinking about taking away his computer. I wanted to ask you about that: Do you agree that would be the thing to do to punish him?"

I was flabbergasted that they would think of taking away the one thing that Lewis expressed any feeling for, that gave him any pleasure, and that served as the basis for the little social contact he had. They seemed to have no sense of the impact of their actions upon Lewis.

I tried to say this to the Perrys, but Dr. Perry interrupted me by saying, "Well, I see you are one of those psychologists who don't believe in discipline," and that was the end of that discussion.

"I am concerned about Lewis," I said as the discussion collapsed into a strained silence, "and I want to do some psychological testing to help get a better picture."

"I knew it was going to come to that," Dr. Perry said with a hint of triumph in his voice. "When my wife said we were going to see a psychologist, I read up a little on what psychologists do, and I read about psychological testing. There is a lot of research questioning the validity of psychological tests, is there not, Doctor?"

I felt like I was back in school.

"Yes, but as an ancillary to the process of clinical judgment, they clearly have their place," I replied in my coldest and most rational tone.

"Are you recommending this because you think there's something wrong with our son?"

"I am recommending this because the school has expressed concern and I agree with their concern and want to find out as thoroughly as I can if there is any problem."

"The school is only concerned because they think he should be sleeping around at his age," Dr. Perry retorted, reducing the issue of Lewis's obvious social isolation to one of not being sexually active.

"You are asking for my professional opinion and that of Lewis's teachers," I said coldly. "I think he needs testing and most likely therapy."

"But that's only your opinion, you really don't have any scientific proof to back you up, do you? We have taught our son never to say anything unless he can prove it absolutely, and we certainly would not want him subjected to tests of doubtful validity unless there was solid proof they were needed and would help."

With that Dr. Perry got up and left the room; Mrs. Perry stood, shook my hand, thanked me for seeing them, and left. I never got a chance to say good-bye to Lewis. I wrote them a letter reiterating my concern but never heard from them again. Only later did I realize that no one in the family referred to the others by name, only by role.

The psychological problems we face are also social. Disconnection is pervasive in our society for several reasons. A culture of individualism exalts autonomy above the connecting fibers of tradition, community, or society. At a deeper level the ethos of control and detachment, when insinuated into family life, produces those false selves who are constantly fleeing from intimacy or trying every desperate ploy to achieve it. Such an upbringing only encourages them to find increasingly ingenious ways to keep others at bay. The exaltation of individuality at the expense of relationship and a narrow-minded reliance on technical efficiency alone can easily take root in personalities deformed by being raised in an atmosphere of detachment. The worship of autonomy and efficiency provides ready rationalizations for these styles of false selfhood.

Raised in an impersonal milieu, the offspring of modernity often lack the psychological resources for authentic intimacy. They are easy prey for the purveyors of counterfeit community.

Jerry's family was the reverse of Teri's. His accountant father and school principal mother provided all the stability a child could want. Chores began every Saturday morning at 8:30 sharp, regardless of whether or not Jerry had other activities that day. The first two weeks of every August, Jerry and his family went to the same cottage on the same lake in upstate New York with the same set of his parents' college friends, despite the fact that none of the other families had children Jerry's age. Right through his senior year in high school, his parents insisted on approving each book Jerry read and every TV show he watched. And every Sunday at 11:00 the family went to church. The pastor seemed to Jerry to have been made in his parents' image: given to using the pulpit for long scoldings sprinkled with quotations from the Bible.

Jerry was a shy and diligent student whose work was neatly done; teachers loved him. He was sent to the state university where his parents met. It seemed like an educational labyrinth compared with his small suburban high school. Lonely and overwhelmed, he took to spending long hours in the student union, drinking coffee and telling himself that the presence of other figures cramped into the booths around him meant human companionship.

Over the weeks he was befriended by an earnest and freckled young woman with a sharp eye for lonely freshmen. She smiled at him over endless cups of coffee, commiserated about the complexities of physics, and invited him to a party at her off-campus apartment.

There he met a dozen or so other friendly young men and women who expressed a genuine interest in where he was from and what his concerns were. They were more than ready to share their struggles adjusting to university life. There were no drugs or overt sex, just a little beer and wine and some hugging and kissing in the corners reminiscent of high school parties in his friends' basements. "At last," he wrote his parents, "I'm finally making some friends in college."

During the party there was even some gentle conversation about God and the Bible without any of the harshness Jerry had learned to associate with religion. It turned out that several of his new friends were going to a conference the next weekend to hear a speaker talk about overcoming guilt and becoming more loving.

Boy, I could really use that, Jerry thought, and it sure feels better to be around real people than to spend any more nights of bad coffee deluding myself that I'm surrounded by compatriots. Besides, these people really care. I finally feel like maybe I belong somewhere. His newfound friend kissed him good night and promised to pick him up next Friday afternoon.

It was several weeks before his parents realized that his letters had stopped coming. Then they received a telegram saying he would not be coming home for the holidays but would be spending Christmas on retreat in rural Vermont. Confused, they called his dorm, but no one remembered seeing him there in the prior few weeks. His parents drove quickly to the campus and spent hours tracking down his instructors, only to discover that his attendance, in the two classes small enough for it to be noticed, had trailed off to nothing. Talking to kids in his dorm, they heard the rumor that their son had joined some group of religious fanatics and had been seen handing out leaflets around the campus.

Just before Christmas a private detective traced Jerry to a farm on the Canadian border. There the detective found a young man rigidly insisting that his parents didn't care about him. Jerry insisted that now he had a new family and would not be going back home. Months later, another man, willing to risk a kidnapping charge, brought Jerry back against his will to his parents' house, just about the time he should have been returning from college for spring break.

When I first saw Jerry, he was sitting in my waiting room shaking his head from side to side as if he were trying to start a motor that had stalled in there. Dazed, he would spend whole sessions staring out my window, barely able to talk. Two summers passed by that window before Jerry could concentrate, reason, gain some direction for himself, and return to school. But even five years later, he occasionally caught himself peering blankly out his window.

OUR FEARS of connection rest on the psychological fault lines of the false self that envisions relationships as either a collapse into dependency or the maintenance of a brittle and defensive autonomy. Many religious, political, and professional cults in our society stand ready to take advantage of those desperate for dependency. On the other hand, the media has a propensity for stories in which intimate relationships are portrayed as either traps or chronic battlefields in which couples coexist like railroad tracks, running parallel but never really touching unless they collide by mistake. Such groups and images appeal to the false self and give our fears of relationship legitimacy, keeping us from seeking an authentic experience of connection with others and with the sacred.

The authors of *Habits of the Heart* call for a return to an emphasis on the common good, a rediscovery of civic involvement and moral concern, and the re-creation of community. However, overcoming our fear of "abandoning our separation and individuation" surely requires more than simply a moral exhortation to be civic minded.

These fears are now deeply rooted in our psyches. Overcoming them often demands a painful process of confrontation and transformation. Gradually the protective aspects of those fears must be faced courageously and given up. This allows our core personality expression. A totalitarian state can be built by people who lack a solid sense of self. The kind community envisioned in *Habits of the Heart*, in which self-concern is put aside for the sake of the common good, can come forth only from people of genuine psychological integrity and maturity. Thus before community can be cultivated, personal growth and maturity must begin.

Likewise many today decry the growing fragility of family relations and mount campaigns to strengthen the family. "Family values" has become a virtual cliché in the speech of every politician running for office, and no magazine article on contemporary America seems complete without a denunciatory reference to the high divorce rate. To the extent that families are broken apart by social and economic policies under public control, such crusades may help.

At a deeper level, the fragility of intimacy (like the bemoaned loss of community) is often a function of our fear, anxiety, and emptiness. Stronger bonds of caring can be erected only on a solid sense of selfhood and on an experience of connection as enhancing rather than as destructive, controlling, or smothering—an experience that seems increasingly rare in our society. Unless individuals can forge mature identities and nondestructive bonds of friendship, love, and parenthood, family life is apt to remain precarious.

Others rail against the decline of organized religion under the forces of materialism and scientific criticism rampant in modernity. Often they call for a revival of traditional religious practices or moralities. These are not the heart of true spirituality, however. The language and practices of the various religious traditions depend upon a more fundamental sense of the sacred, an awareness that life is rooted in a reality beyond itself.

I am not saying that all religions have the same beliefs, for I am not talking about belief at all in the intellectual sense. Rather I have in mind the experience of being in relationship to something greater than ourself. This, in turn, requires the willingness to give ourself over to that more encompassing and cosmic presence. This willingness, in turn, depends upon a sufficiently strong sense of self to tolerate that (and other) connections without feeling engulfed, smothered, or destroyed. Thus a vital and growing spirituality may depend more on the recovery of a vital and growing selfhood than on the revival of any particular religious forms.

Throughout history, religions have given their members the sense that their individuality is tied to something beyond itself, something mysterious and sacred. That larger reality may be a sense of the cosmos and the natural order as intrinsically valuable; it may be a spiritual power that is seen as pervading everything; it may be a transcendent divine plan. Unless we can overcome our fears of connection and recover a truly spiritual sensibility, the language and practices of the particular religions will make little sense. They may carry the memories of tradition or the warmth of fellowship, but they lack spiritual power, the power that transforms lives and cultures, the power that increases our wisdom, the power that gives life lasting meaning.

The loss of community, the fragility of the family and other personal relationships, and the weakening of religion are serious concerns. But they are often addressed in too superficial a way. The restoration of the social fabric, the reclaiming of intimacy, and the recovery of spirituality depend upon renewing our capacity for connection. This requires more than moralistic exhortation, more than the repetition of traditional phrases, more than playing upon our defensive needs for guilt, rebellion, or dependency. These problems are symptoms of the same disease: the loss of our capacity for connection, a loss deeply rooted in our characters and psyches. Thus many of our social problems are also psychological.

Just as individuals go from childhood to adolescence and on to adulthood, so perhaps do cultures. A fused and hierarchical medieval society bears some resemblance to the symbiosis of early childhood. The passionate individuality of modernity is more like the adolescence of Western culture than its adulthood in spite of what the eighteenth-century prophets of the Age of Reason had hoped. Modernity and the discovery of individuality become, like adolescence, a necessary, if costly, stage of development; a necessary stage but not the final one. Culturally, as well as personally, we are now faced with the task of forging bonds of connection that go beyond the totalitarianisms of childhood and the atomistic individualism of modernity—bonds that grow from selves secure enough to join with others, to give themselves away, to nourish others.

But before those mature connections can be forged, we must access and draw on that real self within us, which, in turn, requires the courage to confront the needs, fears, anxieties, and empty places within. One payoff for that valiant struggle to find the real self is the power to live our own, and not someone else's, life.

CHAPTER 6

The Courage to Live Your Life

ONCE AGAIN, as Marion turned the corner, she felt the pit in her stomach. For two years now, every time she came within sight of the red-trimmed ranch house, dread overwhelmed her. What am I going to find today? John passed out on the floor? John promising that tomorrow he'll be out looking for a job? Or John merrily making dinner for me as if nothing were wrong? She mentally ticked off the possibilities, and the hole in her stomach got deeper and wider.

Why do I stay? she parroted to herself the question asked by all of her friends and her several therapists.

Because I love him! she had always answered.

But that answer had broken like a paper clip bent back and forth once too often. How can I love a man I don't respect? she now asked herself. And how can I respect a man who drinks up all the money he's earned from all his patents?

How can I respect a man who's wasting an honor's degree from MIT by being in a stupor most of the time? How can I respect a man who denies that anything is wrong when the ruins of his life litter the floor around him? How can I respect a man who rages at me for hours, spewing nonsense? And (here her internal dialogue took a decidedly nasty turn) how can I respect myself when I stay and let myself be abused? How can I respect myself when I see dreams of children and family slipping away and do nothing to stop it? I'm just as bad, she thought.

At first she had told herself it was love and loyalty and commitment—all those virtues that her mother and the nuns had embedded in her mind through countless repetitions, like a computer program ready to be run as soon as the button of suffering was pushed in her life. That had been mother's way, she recalled. Her father did not drink, but he had several affairs, which her mother endured with martyred resignation and a whiff of moral superiority. Now, after ten years of broken promises and scenes of humiliation, Marion too felt herself ensnared in a mesh of lies and deceptions. To her horror, she had begun to realize that she was acting just as her mother had, making excuses for John and for herself. And she had begun to question whether this really was the way her mother and the nuns had intended her to live.

No, Marion knew it was not virtue but some dark, binding energy deep within that held her in this increasingly narrow orbit. Marion had insisted on keeping her money separate and using it to cover household necessities. She was appalled to realize one day that this attempt to be responsible only maintained John in his habit by providing a roof over his head and food on his table. Nevertheless she stayed with John, continuing to insist on keeping their accounts separate. Once John had demanded her checkbook. Marion refused. In a rage he struck her. Marion had always said, If he hits me, that's it, the final straw, and I'll leave. But that was six months ago, and here she was, still driving up her suburban driveway with a black hole in her gut.

When we first met, Marion's concern was staying with John.

"I've put so much into that relationship," she said to me. "I know it's painful, but I just need some way to manage the pain."

She described the times he embarrassed her at parties: drinking too much and then trying to dance with every woman in the room except Marion, staggering from room to room, interrupting conversations with nonsensical comments, and finally passing out on a bed somewhere. He was too heavy for her to carry, but one or two of the men at the party would usually help drag him to the car; she would drive home and leave him sleeping in the garage. Often she was too humiliated to call or see the hosts again. After ten years of this, her list of friends had dwindled considerably.

Parties at home were better. At least when he passed out, she could leave him on the living room floor.

She had gone to work partly to escape him and partly because she could never really trust him to take care of her or even to contribute to the household. Some royalties still came in on his patents. At first he had worked at consulting jobs, but they had trailed off, and he hadn't looked for work in years. She remembered one of his former professors calling and asking what John was doing. Nothing, she had replied honestly. What a shame, what a waste, he had repeated over and over, and she still recalled the sadness in his voice.

So Marion had gone to work, at first telling herself it was only temporary. Gradually, imperceptibly, she accepted it and later grew to enjoy it. She rose slowly to a minor supervisory position in the import firm where she had started as a bookkeeper. But it was not the life she wanted for herself. She still dreamed of children and a regular family life.

"I'm losing everything," she said to me. "I've lost so many friends because I've been too humiliated by John's behavior to see them again. I feel my plans for a family slipping away. I'm losing respect for myself. I'm too embarrassed to tell people what my life is like. And there's John, on the surface perfectly content and happy. He doesn't have a problem, nothing wrong with drinking and having a little fun, he says. How can you respect a man like that? There's no way to relate to him, nothing to talk about. Yet when I don't talk to him, he gets furious, yells and screams and throws the chairs around and then pours himself a bottle or so and passes out."

Marion's speech trailed off. She sat in silence for a few moments and then continued, "I can hardly get out of bed anymore. Can hardly move or concentrate. Co-workers are telling me how terrible I look. I don't know what to do. People tell me there's no way it's going to get better as long as John drinks, and he shows no sign of stopping. But I can't just throw him out."

"Why not?"

"It wouldn't be right."

"Because?"

"He can't take care of himself. He's sick, he has an illness. He needs help."

"What happens to the rest of your life?"

"I don't know, I just don't know. You have to help me accept it. You have to help me find ways to deal with it."

"I can't."

"What do you mean, you can't? That's your job."

"It's not my job to sit by and watch people destroy themselves. It's my job to help people change, but they have to meet me at least part of the way. I can prescribe medication, but I can't take it for you. You want John to change, but it's not clear that he wants to change. I want you to change because I see the pain your life is causing you, but it's not clear you want to change. You're sitting on a hot stove and want me to prescribe painkillers for you. I can't in good conscience do that. The only cure for someone burning their behind on a hot stove is to help them get off it."

As I told her that, I saw a flush of anger and embarrassment suffuse Marion's face. "I want understanding, I want support, not to be picked on," she cried out. Then she remembered the advice her priest had given her about John. "All he needs is a little love and understanding," Father McBurn had said. Ten years of love and understanding and John was still passed out on the floor. And besides, she found out later, Father McBurn had to be transferred by the bishop because of his own drinking problem. Maybe he was speaking about himself, she thought. Maybe love and understanding are what he felt he needed. But it hasn't really helped John. Would it really help me? she wondered. She got up and left the office early and did not come back.

Instead she went to a therapist recommended by a friend. She explained the situation and what she wanted, and he agreed to her terms. He would not confront her about John's drinking and her marriage. For six months they worked together. He was sweet and understanding. She felt better going each week and getting everything off her chest. Her energy came back. She found herself looking in the mirror and wanting to try a new hairstyle and use some makeup again. Her co-workers started to compliment her on how good she looked.

Then one day she came home and found John in a rage. "I need money," he shouted in his slurred and stumbling speech. "Where's my royalty check? It's supposed to come this month!"

"It came and I put it in the bank, as we agreed," Marion said.

"You bitch! Who are you to control my money? It's my money!" he screamed. Furious, he struck her.

"I'm going to the bank!" he yelled, grabbing his jacket and running to the car. Fortunately he couldn't find any keys in the jacket. He slammed his fist on the wheel with such force that the whole car shook. Then he rolled slowly sideways and passed out on the seat.

"Oh my God," Marion thought, standing in the doorway, "nothing has changed."

The next day she made an appointment to see me.

"Why did you come back?" I asked.

Marion described the latest scene of John's anger. As she talked, the feeling of desperation rose within her.

"I'll do anything," she said, "anything to get free of this prison. I'm willing to learn whatever I need to learn. I'll let the chips fall where they may."

"Marion," I asked, "what do you want from me?"

"I want you to help me."

"Help you do what?"

"I don't know. I know I should leave John, all my friends tell me so and I know you think so. My mind says go, I can't take this anymore. This is not a marriage, it's a battleground, it's a prison, it's a tomb. Whatever was there has died. Dead and gone. And I'm dying too. But something inside me says, You can't leave him, he needs you, and you took vows when you married him. That was your choice, you freely chose to marry him, and now you're stuck with that choice. Nobody said it would be easy. Round and round those two voices go. And I just don't know what to do."

"What do you want to do?" I asked again.

"I don't know, I just told you, I don't know. I have all these voices inside me. I don't know what I want. I don't even think I know what the question means."

"When you think about asking yourself what you want, what comes to your mind?"

Immediately an image of Marion's mother flashed into her head. She recalled her father's escapades—leaving for work early and coming home late, sometimes not coming home at all. Her mother endured it, but she looked very sad most of the time. That sad look on her mother's face melted Marion. I have to be good, she used to think, I have to make things as easy as possible for mother. So when her brothers and sisters came along, she took charge of them without even being asked. "Such a good girl," everyone said.

When she would come home from school, bursting with excitement about a spelling award or a grade on a paper, her mother would be sitting in a chair staring out the window, preoccupied and sad. Marion wouldn't have the heart to disturb her. If her mother noticed her, most often she would say, "Marion, take care of your brothers and sisters."

In high school her mother had wanted her to be a nurse; the nuns wanted her to join the convent. "I don't know what I want to do," she once said to her school principal, Sister Ann.

"Your duty is to help others," the nun told her. "You should be a sister. Being a nurse is all right, but being a nun is better. You're such a good girl, you should join the convent."

"Why do you want me to be a nurse?" she asked her mother.

"You could live at home," she replied, "and attend nursing school at St. Joseph's Hospital downtown."

"I'm not sure I want to be a nurse."

"It's a good job. Your cousin's a nurse, and she's doing fine. I'm sure you'll like it too."

She once asked her father during one of the few times he was home.

"I don't care," he said gruffly, "do what you want. You'll just get married anyway. Maybe your brother will go to school and be an engineer, but you'll just end up married anyway."

She fulfilled her father's prophecy. Unsure of nursing, she started at the local junior college, taking courses in bookkeeping. At a New Year's Eve party she met the brother of one of her classmates, visiting from New York for the holidays. He was ten years older than Marion and already a successful engineer and inventor. She fell in love. They were married within a year.

What a catch, Marion's mother and aunts exclaimed, such a successful man. Nobody seemed to notice that he got drunk at the reception, and Marion's two brothers had to carry him to the limousine.

Before the wedding they had seen each other only on the weekends when she went to New York or he came up to Boston. Only after she moved to New York did Marion discover what John's life was really like: how much he drank, how disorganized his personal affairs were, and how few friends he had. They bought a small house in the suburbs, but Marion found she had little in common with the neighborhood women. Totally preoccupied chasing toddlers and changing diapers, none of them worked outside the home.

When her mother came to visit, she was ecstatic about the little house. "Just what I've always dreamed of," she said. "I'm so happy for you."

For some unknown reason, Marion did not share her mother's enthusiasm. Instead she had a slightly empty feeling, a hollow feeling that would grow into a bottomless crater over the next ten years.

Only once did she try to discuss John's drinking with her mother. Even at a distance of two hundred miles, Marion felt her mother's voice turn cold and hard on the phone. "What did you expect," she told her daughter, "that marriage would be a bed of roses?"

"It's not hard to understand," I told her after she unrolled this scenario, "why you find it so difficult to discover what you want. No one ever taught you to do it. Everybody had their own ideas about what your life should be. They were so sure they were right that they didn't have to bother learning who you really were and what your life was actually like."

"I see that, but I can't do it. I get furious with myself when I even think about asking myself what I want."

"Furious? What do you say to yourself?"

"It's not right, it's selfish. I feel I'm a selfish person to want anything for me. My duty, as Sister Ann once told me, is to take care of others. She said that because I was so strong and good, I was blessed with the role of meeting the needs of others, something that people who were less good and more selfish could not do."

"So you can't ask anything, no matter how small, for yourself?"

"No. No. A thousand times no!" Marion said with mounting anger. She continued, "When I even *think* about doing anything for myself, a voice inside me says, You self-centered, no-good, ungrateful brat! Who are you to think you deserve something for yourself, worthless, guilty wretch."

"It must be a very painful way to live," I said gently, "to have to beat up on yourself so severely every time you want something. No wonder you never ask for anything if such punishment always follows."

Marion looked stunned—her face blank, her expression frozen. A small trickle of tears appeared. Soon more tears flowed, a steady torrent that brought after it a series of sobs rising from the core of her being and shaking her whole body. Marion left the office clutching a box of tissues, feeling weak and emotionally drained.

"Marion," I asked her at the start of her next appointment, "I've listened to your tale of loyalty to John, loyalty to your mother and her example, loyalty to your tradition. I respect your loyalty; it's a great virtue. But I do have to ask you, What has this life of loyalty cost Marion?"

Marion sat dumbfounded. What has it cost me? she thought. What price have I paid? A flood of questions tumbled into her mind. What sort of question is that? Why ask a question like that? What difference does it make? It's only my life.

What? she stopped in mid-thought.

"Only my life? No, my only life. It's my only life. It's my only life. Why am I treating it so carelessly? Isn't life supposed to be a gift? Isn't it supposed to be sacred? Doesn't that apply to me too? Why doesn't that apply to me? Why is John's twisted life more deserving of consideration than mine? Why is my mother's life of sacrifice and bitterness holier than my life? Why hasn't anyone ever cared enough to consider my life? The nuns were concerned only about preserving their order. My mother was concerned only about keeping me around since she didn't really have a husband. John is concerned only about having a roof to protect him while he gets wasted. Why hasn't anyone ever asked what I'm concerned about or what's important to me? It's not so hard. I can ask what they want; why can't they ever ask what I want?"

No tears. Rather an explosion. "It feels like hell is opening up within me," she said. "I'm on fire. I feel like I'm going to burn everything around me. Why couldn't anyone have cared enough? I can take the time to ask myself what I want; why couldn't anyone else?"

She left the office shaking with fury. She could hardly drive home. She wanted to speed and race and do bumper cars with the others on the road. She drove to a park to calm herself, but everything she tried only stirred her up more. Why?! she kept screaming to herself, Why didn't anyone care? She began to walk, hoping to work off some of the fury. But she found herself almost running around the park, too agitated to sit still.

I can't go home, she realized, I'm too upset. Meg, she thought, I'll go stay with Meg.

She stopped at a pay phone and called her old friend from college who had also moved to New York. From Meg's house she called John and told him she would not be home for several days. "Oh" was all he said; he seemed too drunk to care. Guilt, she thought, I should feel guilty, but all she could feel was rage.

Even after dinner and a few hours talking, she was still pacing back and forth, unable to sit down, unable to concentrate.

The next morning she called work and told them she was sick. It was Friday.

Fortunately she and Meg were about the same size, so she didn't have to go home for clothes. Borrowed jeans and sweatshirts were all she needed. And Meg had a bicycle. Marion set off for three or four hours of furious pedaling across the countryside and returned exhausted but still trembling inside.

Early in our work together, I had asked Marion to keep a journal. "You will need a place to record random thoughts and insights, memories that return, significant conversations, ideas from books and articles you read, a record of new ways of behaving that you're experimenting with," I had told her. "You will find some way of keeping notes—a diary, a notebook, loose scraps of paper in a folder—indispensable, and later you will have a record of your journey to look back on."

She hadn't paid much attention to this request. But now, sitting in Meg's guest room, she found herself reaching for her notebook time and time again. As the memories from childhood overwhelmed her, she wrote them down. As connections struck her between her parents' behavior and her attraction to John, she wrote them down. As she remembered things she'd been told as a child that still influenced her, she wrote them down. And as the pain and grief washed over her, she wrote and wrote and wrote. Notebook after notebook piled up next to the desk in Meg's guest room. Page after page of nightmares, cries of outrage, pain-filled phrases. Page after page. At first the rage had a life of its own, forcing itself into her consciousness almost against her will. As the notebooks piled up, she gradually felt some control returning.

After the weekend she returned home.

"Where have you been?" John demanded, looking up from the television set.

"I spent the weekend with my friend Meg," she replied.

"Oh," John said and went back to watching TV.

After that she barely spoke to her husband. As time passed, their lives grew increasingly separate. Marion spent more time at work and with Meg and a circle of friends Meg had introduced her to.

Often her therapy sessions during this time consisted in her spending an hour reading aloud her most poignant journal entries. She started the sessions sitting down but was unable to remain so. After a few minutes of reading, the agitation would seize her, and she would jump up and pace back and forth across my office, reading passages from her journals.

"It hurts so much inside," she would say. "I feel the anger is tearing my insides apart. Why does it hurt so much?"

A silly question, she thought to herself. My family, my teachers, all ignored or abused me while I was growing up. That's got to hurt. And I've taken right up where they left off, ignoring or abusing myself. And I've let John carry on the same tradition. It's a lot of hurt.

Often the feelings of sadness felt overwhelming. Then Marion would climb on her bike and ride furiously, tears streaming down her cheeks. Or she would write for hours in her journal. Over the months, the pain gradually subsided, and Marion felt her strength returning.

I need a rest, she said to herself, I need to relax my mind and soul. She called and reserved a room in a lodge in the woods. Hiking, she thought, tires the body and relaxes the mind.

But it rained. It was bleak. First torrents washed against the window, then came a steadier, slower rainfall. The kind that lasts all day, she thought, probably all weekend. Planning to hike and rest her mind, she had not packed any books. She had hoped to see a vibrant green and brown forest through her window; instead there was only a dull gray fog. As she watched the rain, the old depression came back.

I can't let this get the best of me, she said to herself, but I know I can't fight it.

She lay on the bed, allowing the black hole to swallow her once more.

Time passed.

Darkness.

Stillness.

She felt so heavy that she could not move her limbs. Death.

Is this death? she wondered. Yes, I'm dying. This is death. I'm going to sink into this emptiness inside me and die. I'm dying. No, death is inside me; I must have already died.

Yes.

The dark, guilt-ridden convent school where God was replaced with a rule book was death. Every time I was scolded or beaten for the most insignificant things—and the only things I did wrong were insignificant things—I died a little.

The home where nobody talked about the obvious things was death. Every time I came home and asked my sad mother what was wrong and she brushed me off with a flat "Nothing," I died a little. Every time I went for days without seeing my father, and every time he refused to answer my questions, I died a little. That house quiet with frozen rage was a tomb.

And living with John is death. Watching someone I love slowly kill himself meant dying myself. Every time his actions humiliated me, every time I lost a friend, every day I stayed, I lost respect for myself and I died a little.

So now I'm dead.

The black cloud inside her merged with the black cloud outside the window, and the boundary between the inner darkness and the outer darkness slipped away. She was engulfed in a paralyzing emptiness.

Then, suddenly, she felt as if electricity had jolted her body.

An overpowering, empowering energy filled every cell. Gripped by a power beyond any power she could consciously summon, she felt sustained by a life coming from a place inside her that she never knew existed. The words "passed from death to life" echoed in her mind. Death and life, she thought, together. A life of slow dyings I've lived, but at the bottom of the black hole, at the base of death, is life. I could throw myself against the world, she said to herself, and not shatter.

Full of life, she grabbed her coat and ran out into the constant, gentle mountain rain.

The world looked different. She felt full of an energy she had never known. And the glistening trees and steady wind pulsed with the same energy. She felt as if she could draw that energy from the trees and wind into herself and merge with it and be empowered by it.

"Boy, are you different," Marion's boss said to her the following week. "I've never seen you look so relaxed. What's changed in your life? Meet a new man?" (Over the years he had learned something of Marion's struggles with John, especially after John had humiliated her at an office party three years ago—the last office party Marion attended.)

"No," Marion said, "nothing's really changed."

But the comment started her thinking. Have I really changed? In the next few months she found herself going home less, feeling less guilty about leaving John alone. Meg had introduced her to a women's support group that met in the neighborhood. Eight women met every other Wednesday night to discuss a book or article they were all reading. Almost immediately Marion had felt a part of this group, and once or twice a week she would go out to dinner with one of the women. It felt good to be doing more on her own.

She felt pretty good as she drove home from those meetings. The chronic pit was hardly there in her stomach.

One night she was surprised that the lights were on all over the house, since John was usually asleep by the time she got home.

Must have passed out, she thought, and left everything on, and then he'll complain about the electric bill.

No such luck. John was sitting up, clearly waiting for her, a glass in his hand and a half-empty bottle on the table next to him.

"You selfish bitch!" he screamed at her. "You're never home anymore. What kind of wife do you think you are? Fooling around on me? Who are you seeing? What's his name?"

It was as if a switch clicked inside her. Maybe it was the contrast between her discussion with her friends and John's tirade. Maybe it was some change that had taken place deep within, beyond her own awareness. In any case, a little voice from somewhere inside whispered, You don't have to take this anymore.

"I don't have to take this anymore!" She echoed the inner voice, but screaming instead of whispering. "Don't talk to me about being a wife until you learn to be a husband. I've wasted the best years of my life trying to be a wife to you. I am simply not going to live this way anymore. You have to leave. Period."

He rose from the chair and lunged toward her as if to strike her. She stepped back and grabbed a heavy wooden sculpture off the table and held it above her head like a club. He lurched forward, tripped over his own feet, and mercifully crashed to the ground unconscious.

Shaken that she had almost clubbed her husband, Marion called the police. In a flat voice she said she had come home and found her husband drunk; he had threatened to hit her as he had before; she had prepared to defend herself but before she had to, he had passed out. She wanted him out of the house. Yes, she said coolly, she would press charges if necessary.

The patrolmen came, dragged John into the back of the black-and-white car, and took him downtown. She felt strangely at peace. No longer upset but calm, she wandered through the house. What a mess, she thought, bottles everywhere. She packed John's clothes in two old suitcases and went to sleep.

John called from the jail as she was dressing for work.

"Explain to them that you're dropping the charges," he said simply.

"I'm not dropping the charges, John."

"What do you mean? Of course you are. You love me, we're married. You can't let your husband rot in jail."

"I will send bail money and money for a cab," she said coldly, "but you can't come back here. A friend's husband is an attorney, and I've already called him. He's drawing up a court order to keep you away from the house. If you come back, it's jail, and I won't bail you out again. I suggest you take a cab to the nearest residential treatment center. They can call me and I'll give them the insurance information. After you've gotten treatment and been sober for a while, we'll discuss our marriage. But as of now, consider us separated, and don't try to come back here. When you're settled someplace, I'll send you your clothes."

Her coldness surprised her. Was it strength? Or was it just that all her feelings had died? It didn't matter. She explained the situation to the officer on duty and wired money from her bank to the station house.

John called her at work from a pay phone, begging her to take him back.

She explained that until she got notification that he was in treatment, she wouldn't talk to him, and hung up.

He called back. She hung up as soon as she heard his voice.

That night a drunk called, saying he was calling for her husband, who had passed out at Matt's Tavern across town. For a moment panic gripped her as an image of John lying bleeding on the sidewalk flashed through her mind. I must get him, she said to herself. Then another voice chimed in. You gave him a chance, money to get help, and this is what he did with it. She gently hung up the phone and went to bed.

A restless night. Dreams of John in his doctoral gown, graduating from engineering school. Dreams of John in his doctoral gown passed out in the middle of a street. Dreams of a midnight call, a trip to the morgue, John dead on a stretcher. She spent the next week back at Meg's house. Gradually the nightmares passed.

Marion found herself restless at work. How many years have I been in this position? she thought. I've lost count. Five? Eight? Who knows? I could be here forever, just like this, supervising a few junior bookkeepers and typing letters. This can't be my whole life.

On the spur of the moment, she went in to see her boss.

"How is my work?" she asked nonchalantly.

"Fine," he replied. "Didn't you read your evaluation from last year?"

"That was last year. This is now. I've put many years in at this company. I know the place as well as the president. I want a raise and a new title and more responsibilities, perhaps as your direct assistant for internal financial affairs or in acquisitions."

"Marion, don't be ridiculous. You don't know about acquisitions and I don't need an assistant. We need you right where you are."

We need you right where you are—the words reverberated through her mind. Her mother needed her right where she was: mother's little aide. She could almost hear her mother say, Don't leave home, go to nursing school and stay home, we need you right where you are. Sister Ann needed a prize student or two to recruit for the convent: Stay here, go to school at the main convent, we need you right where you are. And John's voice joined the Greek chorus in her head: You can't leave me, you can't have a life of your own, you can't have your dreams of family, I need you too much right where you are to take care of me so I can drink and drink. Her whole life flashed before her as she stood in front of her boss's desk. Flushed with anger, she marched heavily out of his office and took the elevator to the office of the president.

"I want to see Mr. Rice," Marion said to his secretary. "I'm Marion Steeples from the bookkeeping department. It will only be a minute."

"I'm sorry, but he's busy. I'm sure you are aware of that."

As if in the grip of a force beyond her control, Marion said firmly, "Please tell him one of his employees wants two minutes of his time."

Rice was a rumpled man, shirt collar open and tie hanging at a skewed angle. His desk was invisible beneath a mound of papers.

"Yes," he said, without looking up from the folder on his desk.

"Mr. Rice," Marion said evenly, "I have worked for you for several years. A dozen bookkeepers have come and gone in that time. I probably know the day-to-day financial workings of the company better than you do. I came here because I needed a job, but now I have to decide on a career, and I'm not going to spend the rest of my life as a bookkeeper. If you want to keep an experienced and valuable employee, we have to discuss a promotion."

Startled, he turned away and looked down at his desk. When he raised his head a few moments later, he told her to return to her department and he would call her the next day.

When she arrived at work the following morning, her boss called her into his office. He could not conceal the surprise in his voice when he said, "The president, Mr. Rice, called at five o'clock yesterday and told me to find a new position for you. He said he didn't want to lose someone with your dedication. I was up most of the night thinking about how to reorganize this department. You'll be supervising those who work with the incoming orders. The other accountants and I will handle the internal company finances."

A week later Marion moved into her new office and began to earn about twice her former salary. Leaving her cubicle in the bookkeeping department for a private office was a bittersweet moment. Excited by the challenge and proud of her achievement, she also knew that the larger paycheck symbolized that she really was on her own.

Two weeks later Marion went to see her parents. She felt the old pit in her stomach as the plane circled Boston harbor and glided down onto the runway. Marion's youngest sister, in her mid-twenties, still lived at home, working as a nurse at St. Joseph's Hospital downtown. Too old to run around, her father was home most of the time. Her parents spent their days sliding past each other with a minimum of friction. "They can go for days," her sister said, "and never speak."

As though it were a cue, as soon as the last morsel of food was consumed, Marion's mother stood up and started to gather the dishes and her father headed for the den and the TV.

"No," Marion said softly, "I want you two to stay here. We have to talk."

"No talk," her father said, standing a few yards from the table, "the game is on."

"Sit down, Dad," Marion said, more forcefully this time.

"Sit down," Marion's mother said, "she probably wants to tell us about John."

"He was a drunken bum," her dad said, still standing.

"I don't want to talk about John," Marion said. "I wrote you that we were separated, and I hardly hear from him, so there's nothing to tell."

"He was a bum," Marion's father repeated, "but he was your husband, and you had no business calling the cops on him and throwing him out."

"I said I don't want to talk about that," Marion replied, looking her father straight in the eye for the first time in her life. "I want to talk about you and Mom."

"No," he said, turning his back on her and waving his hand dismissively. "If you came here to bitch, you wasted your ticket."

"Is that all you can say to your daughter? You can't even give her a few minutes of your precious TV time?" Marion's eyes fixed on the back of her father's head.

He turned suddenly and resumed his place at the table. "OK," he said, "let's have it."

"I'm not here to bitch, and I'm not here to blame, but what I saw when I was growing up taught me a lot. I learned to avoid seeing and saying things, no matter what the cost, and to tolerate virtually intolerable conditions. I learned to expect to be criticized or ignored. I learned not to expect anyone to understand or to care. I was taught that it was selfish to notice what was happening to me and that I existed only to do what others needed or wanted. I believe that's called slavery.

"So that's what I did. I married a man and didn't notice or discuss that he drank too much. I tried to take care of his needs, and he only abused me more, first verbally and then physically. I never asked myself what effect this had on me or what I wanted. So now I'm in my thirties. It may be too late for me to go back to college and train for a real career; it may be too late for me to meet another man in time to have children.

"I'm not angry at you; I'm really not. Sure, in the last couple years I've been furious at you many times. I know you did the best you could, but your teaching and example affected me. And I didn't think about their effect and you didn't think about their effect, and that's the problem, because they did have an effect, and the consequences, even if unintended, have been disastrous."

"Are you finished now?" her father said as Marion fell silent.

"Yes."

"OK. Now you've gotten that off your chest, I'm going to watch the game, and you can go back to New York anytime." With that her father got up and walked into the other room. Without a word, Marion's mother went into the kitchen and began doing the dishes. Marion followed her, and the two women worked in silence. Nothing more was said about Marion's life. The next morning her sister drove her to the airport.

Returning home from Boston, Marion was exhausted but exhilarated. Even if nothing changed with her parents, Marion felt relieved that she had spoken up for herself and had said things that had lain on her mind for months.

As time went on she noticed another change. She found herself going back to church. Not because she had to but because she felt drawn back. That felt different. She hardly ever went to services. Instead at least twice a week she would go when the sanctuary was empty and dark and sit near the back and let herself relax into the flickering candles, lingering incense, statues, and stained glass.

Freed from distractions, she focused her attention on the cross hanging over the altar or the pictures of the disciples painted around the sanctuary. Her body was relaxed, but her mind was alert. The same power she felt that day in the woods seemed to rise up out of the stone floor and fill her as she sat there with the stillness wrapped around her.

Am I praying? she wondered. Not really, she thought. I'm not using words, I'm not addressing any figure. But I am not alone. There is certainly some presence here. That's what I'm doing. I'm just sitting in the presence.

Sometimes she missed the pageantry of the high masses of her childhood with their long processions, pungent incense, and soaring Gregorian chants. But for now, just sitting in that presence was enough.

C H A P T E R 7

The Snares of the False Self

CARL JUNG once said that when a normal human impulse is repressed, it comes out distorted. Anger denied may erupt as explosive violence: the "good" neighborhood boy who goes berserk and beats up his parents. Sexual repression may eventuate in acting out: the moralistic preacher caught in a motel with a prostitute.

Our culture represses the natural longing for spiritual experience. This need does not disappear. It gets expressed in our society in distorted forms: suicidal cults, hate-mongering sects, vengeful and judgmental religious leaders. Such destructive sects and leaders get their power by manipulating our need for meaning and purpose. Since it is often unconscious, this desire of the soul is easily played upon by such groups and demagogues. Whereas authentic spirituality liberates the real self, these spiritual distorters appeal to and reinforce our false selves. In life's spiritual search, one must be aware of the unhealthy and destructive forms that religion can take.

Some religious groups manipulate the feelings of guilt and self-rejection engendered by the false self by holding out a love that is conditioned on perfection—and so is no love at all. I have a tape of a sermon by (I am told) a popular media preacher where he says explicitly that God loves us only if we follow "his" [*sic!*] rules, and if we don't, "He" will eternally cut us off.

Psychologists see the ravages of this kind of conditional "love" within families where offspring are kept continually insecure about whether or not they are really loved. I have heard parents say that they never tell their children that they're loved because it will "spoil" the kids. Such children usually grow up to be rigidly scrupulous and emotionally driven to keep proving they are good and are tormented by the idea that they are never doing enough.

These same traits can be seen in those who belong to religious groups that talk more about divine punishment than about divine acceptance. Their adherents are often rigidly moralistic, constantly striving to prove their moral worth, and overflowing with guilt. Such congregations create the very problem of guilt they claim to be trying to solve.

Such a relentless conscience is reinforced by preachers who continually emphasize the negative over the positive. They are more likely to shout "thou shalt not" than to say "thou shalt." Such demands produce a negative and punitive voice inside us that is more inclined to yell "Don't!" than to say gently "It's OK." These demands are often backed by the threat of withholding or withdrawing the necessities of relationships—love, support, attention, and so on—unless the code is followed. Those who don't obey will not only be punished by their parents but will be forever rejected by God.

Here is the essence of the guilt-producing process: Love and acceptance are withheld unless a certain standard is followed. This point is often (intentionally or not) grossly misunderstood and caricatured. So let me repeat: Self-destructive guilt is produced not by teaching children rules but by giving them the impression that human relationships are contingent upon fulfilling them perfectly.

This is an impression that religions often seem particularly adept at conveying. My own experience has been that many students and clients who come from devout families feel that divine (and often human) love and acceptance depend upon fulfilling certain requirements.

Such conditionalism goes against everything we know about the deepest impulses of the human heart. I am only a finite human parent with a very limited capacity for love, but I cannot imagine my children doing anything so terrible that I would break off my relationship with them and say they were no longer my children. Now, I have worked in maximum security prisons, so I know something about the extent of human degradation. I can imagine children doing things such that they could no longer live at home or attend family functions. But I cannot imagine cutting my children off entirely, refusing to speak to them, not giving them whatever inheritance was due them, not being there for them if they should need me. And even if they should refuse to speak to me, I am confident that I would remain open and waiting to respond if ever they should call.

And if a very limited person like myself can imagine that kind of love toward his children, how much greater should be the love of God, who, we are told, is infinite and eternal.

Some seem to feel that the only way religion can survive is to play on feelings of guilt. I can't count how many sermons I've heard on radio or TV or tracts I've received on street corners that are designed to make people feel guilty. I've long since lost track of how many times I've overheard parents saying to their children, "God will punish you if you keep that up." My heart sinks every time that happens, and I say to myself, There's another atheist in the making.

If this were all I had to go on, I would think of God as an arbitrary and cosmic tyrant with whom I would want as little to do as possible. I am constantly struck by the fact that almost all my students at the university think of God as the cosmic scorekeeper, ready to take note of the least offense. The result is a conscience that is never satisfied and always on the attack. This attack of the conscience upon the self mirrors the attack of the parent upon the child or the preacher upon the parishioner. The result is pathological guilt.

I was driving late one night with the radio as my only companion. The only company it provided between Indianapolis and the Ohio border was a preacher. So for a few hours, I became his unwilling parishioner. He was talking about forgiveness. But as more and more miles and minutes were consumed by his words, I found myself feeling worse and worse. This is strange, I thought, he's speaking about forgiveness, but instead of helping me feel forgiven, he's making me feel guilty.

That experience was many years ago, but I have remembered it often as I have worked with patients from very religious backgrounds. Often they will talk endlessly about the love of God, while their interior world remains virtually barren of love. It almost seems that the more they say their sins have been washed away, the more they feel burdened with sin; the more they swim in the river of forgiveness, the more guilty they really feel. I realized these religions produce the very disease they claim to cure.

GUILT IS one way religious groups can play upon false selfhood; keeping their members constantly anxious is another. Precariousness is built into human life. We cannot see the future. We must make choices but cannot know all the consequences. This predicament arises from our unique place in the cosmos. Unlike the "lower" animals, we are free and must deliberate and choose, yet we are limited and cannot see all possibilities and consequences.

Choice is inherently ambiguous. To choose is to attempt the impossible and bind the future. The future, however, remains stubbornly unbound. If I marry this person, I cannot marry another; yet this relationship may fail. If I have children, I sacrifice some freedom; if I do not, I sacrifice other basic human experiences. If I choose this career or that, if I resign myself to my apparent fate or if I rebel, and so on throughout my life—in every case I must choose without knowing what will really be best in the long run. Thus some anxiety is inherent in human life.

If anxiety becomes intense enough, we flee from it and seek some security to assuage our insecurities. We try to hold onto something in the vain hope that it will procure that desired security. If only I get into law school or medical school, my future will be secure, many of my students reason. If only I marry this person, my life will be complete, others feel. If only I make eighty thousand dollars a year, I'll be safe. If only the United States regains its status in the world, I'll be secure. If only my race or ethnic group gains power, I'll be OK. If only my ideas triumph in the political arena, life will be fine.

Yet we know, consciously or not, that we cannot be absolutely secure. Doctors get sick; lawyers get into trouble: Their practices fail; their patients and clients sue for malpractice. Marriages end; partners change; spouses die. Political ideals are sold out; they triumph imperfectly and through compromise, if at all.

The more we invest in these things, the more we raise them to some ultimate status, the more vulnerable we become to anxiety whenever they are threatened. Taking tests, getting grades, facing entrance exams may paralyze us with the anxiety that we may not make it into professional school and that our dreamed-of security may vanish. When we fight with our partner and it appears the relationship may not work out, we are plunged into despair. When our nation is under attack, our ideas challenged, or our achievements put under scrutiny, we may react with undisguised fury.

Ironically religion often encourages such idolatry rather than pointing us beyond it. Out of their own anxiety, religious groups have embraced and defended as absolute very fallible legal, moral, cultural, or political norms and institutions and have tried to make adherence to them the source of security for their members. Finite, human, cultural ideas and standards have been identified with God's will. In the past men were sent to prison for saying the earth was not the center of the universe, and many a war has been fought with both sides claiming the same god was on their side.

Various religious groups have regarded ancient law codes, the medieval social order, bourgeois individualism, Victorian morality, and the self-interest of nations as absolute and unchanging and as the bulwark of an institution's or an individual's security. When these are challenged, people feel God is threatened.

Religion can enhance anxiety by playing on our fears and focusing attention on the contingencies of life, its shortness and unpredictability, in a destructive way. Some religious spokesmen promise an assurance that does not reassure but only makes anxiety worse by making security dependent upon performance of rites, moral perfection, or doctrinal purity. I recently heard a televangelist spend an entire hour repeating in different ways his idea that God demands perfection and will not accept anything less. God was pictured as a critic who was never satisfied, whose acceptance depended upon a faultless performance. The anxious soul is perfectly aware that it cannot fulfill such heavenly requirements. That preacher's implicit message was that our only choice was to feel terrible about ourselves for our entire life. Rather than being a balm for a broken spirit, such talk only pours salt into our wounds.

Constant anxiety often signals a lack of trust in oneself and God. The root of the word *faith* is the Latin word for trust. An important psychological function of religion has traditionally been to nourish our capacity for trust. The contingencies of life are taken up into a larger context of divine providence or cosmic order: Behind or beneath the randomness of life, the eyes of faith discern a greater love or purpose.

Anxiety is a part of life. When it intensifies to the point of weakening and undermining us, it becomes pathological. Religion may intensify anxiety rather than assuage it, playing on our false selves rather than encouraging the true self.

Along with the intensification of guilt and anxiety, in my experience, many of the emotional troubles of the pious result from repression. Denying feelings like anger and hurt or suppressing sexual desires leads to the need for more and more suppression and control. A student once told me that the truly devout person must smile and be happy all the time. I thought to myself that he should tell that to Jesus on the cross or to the prophet Jeremiah languishing in prison. And I have seen countless adolescents from pious homes ashamed and confused over the first stirrings of sexuality because they'd been told not to have any desires.

Repression only increases the fear that the denied feelings and desires may erupt. This fear is often projected onto the world as a fear of social, emotional, sexual, or intellectual disorder. In response to this perceived threat, order must be imposed, authority asserted, and anything that might make for instability—emotions, ideas, other groups—repressed. The more the threat of chaos looms, the more authoritarian the religion becomes.

Repressive groups deal with problems by denial rather than by generating the faith and trust necessary to confront them. Devotees are often told simply to forget their problems, get involved in some project, work harder, believe, or have a baby. When religion fails to nourish a sense of faith and trust and instead insists on "solving" problems by suppressing them, it turns itself into a pathological distortion of the spiritual life, which is supposed to foster faith, not fear.

Besides the perceived threat of chaos, there are other reasons for a rush to repression within religion. Guilt is assuaged by following rules. Guilt can be avoided by living in a system in which morality is black and white and no ambiguity exists. Identity can be manufactured through acceptance into a dictatorial social movement. Conformity removes the need for fashioning a sense of self. Often authoritarian groups rush into the emotional vacuums of the present day and fill them with rigid codes and prefabricated identities.

These congregations appeal to the false self's need for submission with demands that crush our autonomy as effectively as totalitarian political systems. I had a client who belonged to a church—not a secret cult but a regular church—that dictated how he should dress, what music and books he could enjoy, and told him over and over that choice was an invention of the devil. The price of belonging to this fellowship was to remain forever a little child who must be continually told what to do.

Such authoritarianism is not necessarily unhealthy. It is no accident that many drug addicts and dropouts from society have been reclaimed most successfully by the Black Muslims, very fundamentalist Christian groups, or very disciplined Eastern religions. Such sects provide an external structure in which the self can function and grow when it lacks much structure within itself—just as clearly delineated boundaries are necessary for the young child.

Psychologically these structures are temporary, designed to let the child's self develop until it outgrows them. Most such religious organizations, however, do not allow their converts to outgrow their dependency upon these authoritarian systems. Rather than seeing such measures as temporary, therapeutic expedients, these groups often seem to keep their members permanently fixed in a state of dependency, providing no incentive to grow beyond it. And often when members do grow up and seek appropriate adult autonomy, they are forced to leave.

Thus an infantile style can often be found in those who seek a protected life, free of the responsibilities of growing up. Such responsibilities bring pain but also growth. In my experience, members of dictatorial religious and political cults often have trouble deciding for themselves what to do. Even after they leave, they try to make everyone into an authority figure. They look to therapists, teachers, or friends to give them the answer rather than to help them discover it for themselves. Also, devotees of such religions have great trouble managing ambiguity and can make decisions only when the issues are seen as black or white.

Change or responsibility may propel people into childish dependency. Some religions encourage this infantilism by unrealistically holding themselves out to uncertain souls as representatives of eternity, bastions of stability where change does not take place. Those who join authoritarian religious or political groups in the naive hope that the responsibilities of living in a world of change can thus be avoided usually react with hostility against the religion when change finally invades the sanctuary, much as a child reacts when its parents let it down. When the Roman Catholic Church began worshiping in modern languages instead of Latin, and introduced contemporary music into its services, self-styled "traditionalists" angrily broke away and tried to start their own churches. When the Episcopal church in the United States voted to ordain women, those newly ordained were harassed and called despicable things by church members who disagreed with the decision.

The price one pays for this modicum of security is the suppression of all individual initiative. Such suppression inevitably builds up a certain amount of hostility. Dependent people are often resentful and hostile. They feel they must smother any vitality and individuality in order to remain dependent, and they resent it. Religious groups may provide a sanctioned outlet for this hostility by directing it toward those outside the group—other faiths, those seen as less moral, or other races or nationalities. People within authoritarian, legalistic religious regimes may discharge the hostility born of dependency through prejudice or self-righteous condemnation of others or by launching crusades. The release of this anger may be a secondary benefit of belonging to these communities.

Such cults are often ruled by a strong figure or set of beliefs or moral law. Strong authority figures demanding perfection create guilt in their devotees. That guilty conscience then can be appeased by identifying with the same strong authority figure—the group, the leader, or some moral or doctrinal code. If I am driven by guilt, feeling that I am among the right people, believing the right things, or living by the right code can mean that I am really all right myself.

Religion can keep people emotionally weak and dependent, diminishing their real self and manipulating their false selves by intensifying guilt, arousing anxiety, and keeping them suppressed and controlled. The erosion of identity, the encouraging of infantile dependency, the discharge of hostility are some of the psychologically and spiritually destructive effects that religion can engender by playing on people's false selves rather than providing the kind of spiritual experience that strengthens the real self.

While most religions talk of dying to self, ironically some keep us stuck in the coils of our own egotism. They are really appealing to our false selves rather than helping us move beyond them. The false self makes us feel like helpless and dependent children constantly needing to be compliant to every parental whim, or like guilty and evil creatures living in constant fear of rejection. And many sects have a stake in keeping those feelings alive in us rather than freeing us from them.

Some religions appeal directly to our selfishness with promises of what we can get out of religion in this life or the next. As I write this I have in my hand a tract a student gave me at the university that declares in capital letters, "SAVE YOURSELF," promising me eternal bliss and happiness and earthly prosperity if only I accept the creed of the tract's author. A slicker promotion and more blatant appeal to my selfishness was never devised on Madison Avenue.

The only death to self that truly sets us free is one that brings us through the wilderness of dying to the false self (and to the inauthentic religious appeals based on it) and to the actualization of the real self, which is capable of mature love and connection. Psychotherapy and spirituality both involve the seed of false selfhood falling to the ground and dying. Ironically this is a dying to the very false selfhood that is the foundation of so much religion.

CHAPTER 8

Leaving Home, Growing Up

WHEN WE have established a solid sense of self, the currents and tides of relationships cannot drown our individuality. We can experience connections that go beyond either a stultifying dependency or an isolating atomism, relationships that preserve both intimacy and individuation.

The same process is at work in our spiritual search. When the real self experiences the union with God that transcends ordinary consciousness, that union is not a spiritual uniformity in which our separate identities are homogenized into a bland religious mass. Rather a connection with the divine is experienced *and* our individuality is maintained. Healthy religious experience, built upon the real self, supports the integrity of the individual while maintaining the connection to a larger sacred reality.

How is it possible to balance the drive for connection with the need for individuality?

Everything from the smallest particles that make up the physical world to human beings to stars and galaxies can be regarded in two ways: as unique individuals and as members of a greater whole. Psychological health requires a balance between our existence as individuals and as parts of larger groups. A mature relationship, or a healthy organization, maintains this balance—neither subsuming the individual parts into the greater whole nor fragmenting the individual parts into disconnected atoms.

This principle can be understood in terms of boundaries: A relationship or community or organization must have adequate boundaries in order to maintain its integrity, and the individual members must have adequate boundaries in order to maintain their identities. As therapists who work with families and couples know, negotiating and maintaining this balance is a major dynamic in most relationships. Never static, the balance of autonomy and intimacy within a relationship is constantly in need of fine-tuning.

The same principle that applies to families and friends applies to societies and to our relationship with God. The maintenance of boundaries provides a criterion for evaluating the health of interpersonal relationships, organizations, and religious experiences. Pathological religion, as discussed in the previous chapter, undermines the real self through the crushing imposition of demands, the erosion of selfhood by guilt, or the swallowing of the self by an engulfing community. Such religions do not respect the psychological and moral integrity of the individual.

Authentic spiritual and psychological transformation involves shedding the false selves and recovering the true self. The development of true selfhood that can maintain its integrity while remaining in relationship is not, however, a simple process. Children start off in relationship, separate in order to constitute an individual identity, and are then able to reconnect at a higher level where that identity is maintained. Breaking away in order to forge our own identity, we return lest we become isolated in our autonomy.

This is not a once-and-for-all event but a continual movement. We may leave our family as a rebellious adolescent and return as a nascent adult. We may have to leave and return many times before that adult relationship is firmly established. Our first love is usually heavily overlaid with symbiosis, defensiveness, and the fear of loss of self. There will usually be many leavings and joinings before we and the others in our life gain the capacity for mature connection outlined here. And even within a relationship there will inevitably be times of closeness and times of distance. Fortunate is the relationship that is strong enough to contain this process and not break. Sadly, not all relationships can.

FLORENCE LEFT home at eighteen. Her brothers got attention; she was treated as if she didn't exist. Their father's old-world mentality dictated that boys went to college but girls became wives and mothers as soon as possible. Or, if they did not marry young, they were expected to work menial jobs to support the boys' schooling. The day after her high school graduation, without a word, Flo took her diploma and moved halfway across the country to live with her mother's sister.

Flo worked days and attended the local junior college at night. She did so well academically that, having earned her two-year degree, she enrolled at the state university on full scholarship and was later accepted at the university's law school. There she met another aspiring lawyer named Mike and soon moved in with him. Five years later, Flo became pregnant, and she and Mike began to plan a wedding.

Should she invite her parents and brothers?

In the decade or so since she had left, she had rarely thought of them. Or so she said. Her aunt had kept them informed of Flo's accomplishments, but no phone calls, cards, or letters of congratulation had arrived on any of her graduations, nor on her passing the bar exam or joining a major firm. Flo had considered herself dead to them and them to her.

Happily pregnant and a bride-to-be, Flo found herself thinking of them more.

"Something inside me says I have to make peace with them now," she said to me on her first visit.

We worked on how she might do this. She wrote them a long letter, describing Mike and their relationship and enclosing pictures and a wedding invitation.

No response.

Her aunt called Flo's parents and tried to talk to them. They refused to discuss Flo with her. Apparently all they had told their friends and relatives back home was that Flo was living with a man and expecting an illegitimate child and was no longer their daughter.

Infuriated, Flo stopped trying.

When Michael junior was two, Flo was back in my office. "I can't believe my parents don't want to know their only grandchild," she told me.

One of her brothers had been married briefly but was divorced after less than a year. The other showed no inclination toward committing matrimony. The irony was not lost on either Flo or me. She, the black sheep, was the only one that was really fulfilling her parents' dream for their children of a career, marriage, and grandchildren.

She wrote them again, sent more pictures.

Again, no response.

As we talked it became clearer that she needed closure, even if they didn't. The wedding invitation and baby pictures had been sent because she felt they wanted to be included. Obviously they didn't feel the same. But she needed some contact with them even if they didn't need it with her.

She and Mike and the baby arranged to fly to her hometown. She sent her parents a letter saying they were coming but, as usual, received no response. She and Mike took a hotel room in town and called.

Her mother answered, sputtered, and put her father on. He hung up.

They drove to the house where Flo had been born and where her parents still lived. On the way over she panicked.

"We can leave anytime," Mike reassured her.

She broke down and cried. They stopped the car, and she composed herself. They pulled into the driveway with their stomachs in knots. Even Michael Junior was exceptionally quiet, perhaps sensing that something significant was about to happen.

They rang the bell.

Flo's mother opened the door.

"Hello, Mother," Flo said evenly, "this is your grandchild."

Little Michael's grandmother screamed and retreated into the void within the living room.

Flo's father appeared out of the dark interior of the house.

"Michael, this is your grandfather," Flo said, pushing the child toward the hulking figure filling the door frame.

"Go away," he said, and he closed the door on the child and his parents.

They retreated to the car and returned to their hotel.

Flo called her brother. Both brothers still lived at home. One was inching toward a college degree at night while selling shoes at a local store. Flo had his work number from her aunt.

He was aloof and unemotional on the phone.

"I never believed you'd do it," he said. She told him where they were staying and how much she wanted to speak to her parents and have them all meet her husband and son.

"I'd love to," her brother said, "but Dad would kill me."

As they were hanging up, he suddenly blurted out, "Is it true what Aunt Lori says, that you're a lawyer?"

"Yes," Flo replied coldly, "and so is Mike." She hung up.

The three of them went out to supper, then took a walk in a park where Flo used to play. Now she was there swinging her son on the same swings she had enjoyed. She felt resigned and dead inside.

The next morning her mother called.

"If your father knew I was doing this, he wouldn't speak to me for a month," she said, "but he thinks I'm out shopping and I just had to call."

Flo couldn't stop the lump from forming in her throat or keep it from growing and growing until she could barely whisper. They met at the park. Flo's mother pushed Michael junior on the swing, and the two women tried their best to catch up on each other's lives. Nervous about the time, Flo's mother left after half an hour.

After that, about every other month, Flo received a letter from her mother concealed in a letter to Flo's aunt. And Flo would include a note to her mother with her aunt's replies. It was the best they could do.

At Michael junior's next birthday, a present came with a note from his grandmother. Two years later the note was from both of his grandparents. Flo never knew whether her father was aware of this or whether it was part of her mother's subterfuge, for he died the following year.

At the funeral, Flo's mother introduced her as "my daughter, the lawyer from New York."

THROUGH THE process of joining and separating again and again we learn to establish our identity in relation to others. The ebb and flow of closeness and distance maintains the dynamic balance between autonomy and connection. Times of separation undergird our individuality; times of connection keep us related to those around us. Alone, we strengthen our interior resources; connected, we sustain and are sustained by others. Of course even when we're alone, we carry the imprint of others inside us; and when we're being most intimate, our uniqueness is not lost. But it's the rhythm of solitude and communion that enables us, over time, to maintain the vital balance of identity and intimacy on which the real self thrives.

This pattern of going out and returning turns up in a wide variety of places. The Greek philosopher Plotinus, for example, sees the cosmos arising and separating from its spiritual source and then returning and reuniting. The contemporary Jewish philosopher Martin Buber describes a process of moving away and returning as central to the life of all relationships, including that of the self and God. "The universe," Buber writes, "expands into its own existence and then returns to be in relationship with God."

Within any relationship between parents and children, between lovers, between siblings, between men and women and their God, there will be times of going apart and times of return. Fortunate is the relationship that is flexible enough to allow this process to occur and to grow as the partners in it grow.

Mature spirituality involves the same pattern. A faith of our own may require leaving the faith of our family, wandering in our own spiritual wilderness, and reconnecting to our family's faith (or perhaps another)—but at a more personal level.

Sometimes I hear parents complain that their sons and daughters "lost their faith" while in college. The faith these young men and women lost was not theirs but somebody else's: They lost their parents' faith, not their own. To have a faith of their own, they must first gain some distance from the one they received from somebody else. Again, we are fortunate if we find or grow up in a faith that is flexible enough to contain this process and allow us to progress within it.

Amy was raised in a traditional Jewish family. She watched her two older brothers celebrate their bar mitzvahs, the elaborate ritual initiating them into the people of Israel. But no such rite of confirmation and identity was available to young women in her extremely orthodox congregation. As much as she loved the family seder and the candles of Hanukkah, in college she found herself drifting farther and farther away from her Judaism. Living close enough to join her family for celebrations and holiday rituals, she participated in them with a deep and nameless sadness in her heart.

She graduated and married a young man named Jeff from a much less traditional background. He rarely attended synagogue, but she could not even walk by one without that faint but insistent grief grabbing her. So, much to her brothers' and parents' shame, she simply stopped any traditional practices.

Jeff received a promotion, and as a result Jeff and Amy moved away from the city of their birth. One Saturday morning, while shopping downtown in their new city, Amy happened by a synagogue. She froze in midstride—the rabbi's name on the synagogue door was that of a woman.

As if in a trance, Amy wobbled up the stairs and sat in the back row. As fate would have it, a service of initiation was taking place, and both young men and young women were reading from the elaborate scroll. Amy collapsed against the back of the pew in sobs, crying out years of exclusion by her own people.

She found herself going back again and again, making friends with the rabbi, a woman about her own age. At first the less traditional service was strange to her, but the more she learned about this more liberal version of Judaism and the more she grieved for her prior exclusion from her religion, the more at home she felt.

After a year there Amy got up her courage to ask the rabbi if she could have her own service of initiation. She invited her parents and brothers to her bat mitzvah, but they refused to come. They regarded her new community with disdain.

Amy was not surprised; she knew her family well and long before had accepted that they would never change. Because it repeated the earlier rejection of her, their refusal to be with her brought a momentary pain. But surrounded by Jeff, her new rabbi friend, and others from the congregation, she felt exhilarated by the service, healing as it did a wound of twenty years' duration. Six months later she applied for rabbinical school.

LIFE BEGINS with the attachments and dependencies of infancy. Later the child separates, establishing her own identity. She is then, hopefully, capable of relatedness at a new level where selfhood is maintained and not lost. We continue to need times of separation to forge and maintain our identity. A healthy relationship contains this pattern of distance and closeness without breaking. Such times of separation and further individuation are not breaks or breakdowns in a relationship but rather parts of the dynamic life of connection.

In contrast to some schools of modern psychology that make separation the goal of life, I have suggested that our autonomy depends upon relationships. The child moves from relative dependency to relative autonomy, supported by the love and encouragement of significant people in her world. The adult's accessing and strengthening of real selfhood, through greater self-knowledge and authentic self-expression, occurs in a milieu of caring relationships. Dependence and independence are not antitheses but rather points on a continuum. At any one time our life may emphasize independence or connection, but that does not mean we have lost touch with the opposite pole. Any move toward independence occurs in a relational context, and we bring our individuality to all intimate unions.

The same is true of the relationship with God. Times of ecstatic closeness and the felt presence of God are balanced by times of doubt and distance. The core of spirituality is an experience of connection in which identity is maintained and the real self is not lost, absorbed, or overwhelmed. This pattern of separation and reunion keeps the human-divine encounter (like any human encounter) from resulting in a loss of self. Such times of distance, separation, and doubt do not represent spiritual failure or loss of faith; they are in fact essential in any relationship in which real selfhood is sustained.

Religion can promote a self-destructive dependency by appealing to a false selfhood. Some may conclude that therefore any dependency on a universal, transcendent, sacred presence or power is unhealthy. However, since autonomy and dependency are not opposites but parts of any mature relationship, experiences of spiritual union or dependency can sustain, and do not have to submerge, the real self. The continuous process of separating and reuniting, individuating and reconnecting, ensures that our individuality will not be lost or absorbed in the other.

C H A P T E R 9

Deep Inside My Soul

OVER THE last few months, Bob had found it harder and harder to get out of bed in the morning. He remembered wistfully the times he couldn't wait to get to the office: how proud he felt every time he drove up to the building and saw the freshly lettered sign—"Robert Orson, M.D." Arriving before the receptionist, the nurses, and his partner, he would walk through the quiet catacombs of laboratories, examining rooms, and offices and savor the sensation of having fulfilled his dream.

He could also vividly recall, even before that, being the youngest physician named to a team perfecting a new form of eye surgery that literally restored sight in certain types of partial blindness. He remembered the excitement of a ten-year-old girl, whirling and dancing and touching everything in sight when her world came into focus for the first time. And the tears in the eyes of her parents, who barely spoke

English and couldn't stop shaking his hand and choking out their thanks. They still sent him pictures of their daughter on her birthday. Yes, he remembered thinking just a year ago, What could be more fulfilling than giving people back their sight?

And now. And now, only a few years out of medical school, he was gradually having to face the fact that the practice of ophthalmology was losing its fascination. He and his partner had performed the miraculous procedure hundreds of times. Is this, he wondered, all there is to life? Am I condemned to an endless sentence of the same examination repeated a million times? of assembly-line operations? of a growing stack of unopened journals piling up next to my desk?

Driving home one day after work, Bob's head was full of images of the other physicians in his building. There was Brodsky, the orthopedic surgeon on the next floor, who went for three- or four-day junkets to Las Vegas every month. There was White, the radiologist, who took his nurse out for two or three hours almost every day. And there was his own partner, Fred, dipping into the narcotics cabinet to get through the day. What's happening to all of us? he thought. I surely don't want to end up like that.

He knew that his wife, Marsha, had noticed him becoming increasingly distant. A year ago she had listened intently as he recounted over dinner the details of his surgical exploits. He had seen that excited look on her face gradually vanish as he spoke less and less about his work. Absorbed in the responsibilities of motherhood, she had at first seemed oblivious to the change. She had plenty to tell him about the antics of their two toddlers—a boy and a girl only a year and a half apart—and her maternal enthusiasm slowly replaced the events of his day as the focus of their dinner conversation. Usually he just listened in silence.

He knew it was only a matter of time until his growing unresponsiveness weighed on her enough for her to confront him with her concerns. That dreaded moment finally arrived. One night, after supper, she demanded to know what was wrong.

"Well," he started hesitantly, "something's been on my mind the last few months. . . ." Slowly but inexorably his doubts and fears and depression tumbled out.

His wife looked aghast. He could feel panic radiating from her as she said, "But you don't mean you're thinking of quitting medicine? Your patients depend on you. Your colleagues depend on you, the whole hospital staff looks to you and Fred, no one else around does what you do. And I, we—the children and I—depend on you too."

The last, he feared, was her real concern, but he heard the voice of truth behind his wife's anxiety. She's right, he thought, it's not just me. I am part of a net of responsibility, and I can't just abandon it. Besides, I haven't said anything about quitting; I've just expressed some questions, but she jumps to the most extreme conclusion. Is she hearing something behind my words that I'm not even aware of? Or is she letting personal feelings control her response? In any case, Marsha's right, people depend on me. And if I'm honest, I have to admit that I like that feeling.

"No," he reassured his spouse, "I'm not thinking of quitting medicine. These are just some thoughts I've been having lately."

The next day Bob found it even harder to get up and go to work.

"How is it possible," Bob asked me sometime later, after telling me the same story he told his wife, "for the most stimulating and rewarding of professions to turn to dust?"

That question stayed with him for months. In addition there was the loneliness at work and at home. Fred and the other doctors in the building made it clear they wanted nothing to do with such discussions. Fred responded derisively when Bob told him he was discussing it with a psychologist.

"You're not really seeing a shrink, are you?" Fred said in disbelief. "Take a vacation, or if it gets really bad, take Prozac," was his advice. Fred would mock him in the hallways if they were alone by rolling his eyes and pointing to his head in a gesture implying Bob was going insane.

Marsha too shied away from the topic. If Bob brought up his questionings, a bad dream from the night before, or his visits to me, she would pointedly change the subject. When he confronted her, she replied honestly, "I want to be supportive, but really I'm scared. You're not the man I married, the self-confident, almost cocky, doctor. I don't recognize you anymore. You seem more brooding, introverted. No, I can't fathom what's on your mind. I don't understand you. We have everything we've worked for, and now I'm afraid you're going to ruin it somehow. We have all the things we said were important ten years ago when we met—successful career, loyal marriage, healthy children. How can you feel dissatisfied? Have I let you down?"

Bob continually reassured her it wasn't her fault, and she didn't really believe it was. She had done everything just as they had planned and was, in fact, loyal and caring. But they seemed to be growing apart despite their best efforts to stop it.

Bob knew he was putting his wife and family under a lot of pressure. The last thing I want to do is hurt the people I care most about, he thought, but I feel powerless to stop the questions flooding my mind or fight the heavy cloud that engulfs me. I guess I could take pills, but they won't answer my questions.

"How did I get into this mess?" Bob asked me during one of our sessions.

"How did you decide to be a doctor?" I asked in return.

"That certainly seems like a reasonable question," he replied, "but it feels foreign to my mind. Decide to be a doctor? High school? No, not really. College? I was already pre-med. When *did* I decide?

"In subtle ways my parents put pressure on me. They made it clear that I would succeed academically and materially and make them proud of me. Nothing overt, just snide comparisons about how much more intelligent I was than the other kids. And when I would describe a teacher or school counselor I really liked, or a famous scientist, my father's response was always, 'If he's so smart, why isn't he rich?'

"Science came naturally to me. I could read the chapter in the textbook once, grasp the basic principles immediately, and ace the test. Teachers would compliment me by saying, 'You're smart enough to be a surgeon.' And in high school, as soon as I excelled in science, teachers, aunts and uncles, and my father began to call me 'the doctor.' When asked what I was going to study in college, I began to say reflexively, 'Pre-med.' And, of course, everyone would nod approvingly and go on about how wonderful that was and weren't my parents proud? No one ever responded by asking, 'Why?' The answer seemed so obvious.

"In college I immediately felt the comfortable blanket of prestige that warms the souls of pre-med students and prepares them for life after medical school. And the weight of responsibility began to constrain me to that path as I watched classmates struggle over organic chemistry and physics, subjects that came almost naturally to me.

"Of course, I always enjoyed acting. Deep inside my soul, I harbored fantasies of a career on the stage. But looking back I realize that I had been carefully taught to play it safe, to watch out for the inevitable rainy day (one of my father's favorite phrases), and that only a fool would give up a sure ticket to wealth and power for a long shot in theater.

"Yes, I occasionally had doubts back then. But who am I, I would ask myself, to casually give up rewards for which others are killing themselves? So I went off to medical school, was immediately adopted by the fraternity, and here I am."

"It doesn't really feel like a decision at all," I reflected, "more like a foregone conclusion."

"Right, it wasn't my decision. I never really made up my mind to go to medical school. I never really considered alternatives. It was more like following a path from marker to marker without ever considering the destination. Now I've arrived at the end of the trail, and I'm not sure I like it."

I guess I wasn't very responsible, he thought to himself while driving home from therapy, going to medical school when I had no idea what I was doing. Now I'm stuck with Marsha and the kids and the practice. Stuck! That's what I've been feeling. That's what that gloominess is, feeling trapped. What I used to love—wife, family, work—now feels like prison. If they weren't there, I'd be free. But no, they're really victims of my irresponsibility. They thought they were getting a doctor for a husband, father, colleague; but in my soul I really wasn't committed to medicine. It just fell into my lap, and I took it without thinking. So I never did commit myself to it. But now I have it.

"How can I make the best of my medical career?" Bob asked at our next session.

"What does that mean?"

"I don't know. It's not really what I want to do. I was led along by others. I feel like such a fool. I always saw myself as the strong leader type, but in reality I was just being pulled along by the opinion of others and the opportunities they presented to me, like a dumb horse following a carrot."

With individual patients he was fine, and his surgical hand was as steady as ever. But as soon as the last patient left or the surgery was done, Bob ran from the office or hospital. Direct contact with helping people felt fine, but he couldn't stand anyone thanking him or telling him that he did a great job.

"Bob's really gotten distant," he overheard friends say to Marsha. "Is he all right? Mid-thirties is too young for a midlife crisis. What's happening?" But she could only shake her head—she had no idea either.

"What am I going to do?" he asked me in desperation.

"Can you see yourself doing the same thing ten years from now?" I asked. "If you try to visualize it, what do you see?"

"No," Bob replied violently. "No." In his mind's eye he saw himself moving slower and slower: walking in slow motion, greeting patients in slow motion, operating in slow motion, his body feeling heavier and heavier, his life grinding to a halt.

"I just can't do it," he said at the end of the session.

Driving home he asked himself, What can I see myself doing in ten years? The theater suddenly flashed before his eyes. He was on the stage, playing an angry middle-aged man. The emotion in his fantasy performance was palpable, the audience totally absorbed in the action. That's it, he said to himself, that's what I have to do.

"I'm quitting," Bob announced the next week. "I'm selling my practice and moving to New York and entering acting school."

There was a vehemence to his words that shocked me.

"Bob," I said slowly, "are you sure you've thought this through? We've been talking about what you need to do to balance your life more, not about throwing it all over."

"I don't want to supplement my life with acting. I want that to be my life."

"What's Marsha's response?"

"I haven't told her yet; I'm telling you first."

"Bob, it sounds like your mind is already made up and nothing's going to stop you. I know I can't stop you, and I don't even want to, but I think we should talk about other alternatives to make sure this really is the best one. Medical school was not really a carefully considered decision. I don't want to see you do the same thing again."

"No, I've talked long enough. I have to do something, now." Bob stood up and walked out of the room, slamming the door behind him. He sent me a check in the mail but didn't call or come back.

He drove home from my office and abruptly told his wife. Marsha recoiled in shock. She simply couldn't absorb it.

"You don't really mean it," she kept saying over and over. "You don't really mean it."

"I do," Bob insisted coldly. "The practice is up for sale, and I've already enrolled in an acting school in New York."

"But isn't there a compromise? Can't you do something in the community theater? You used to talk about doing community theater."

"I can't compromise with my life. Besides, *now* you want to talk about the community theater. When I brought it up last year, you didn't like the idea. You were afraid it would take away from my time with you and the kids."

"I was afraid of that. But I didn't know then how important it was to you."

"It's too late. I've sacrificed occasional roles in that community theater to the demands of medicine. I can't do it anymore. Medicine has to go. I don't know how I'd live with myself if I went through life without ever knowing if I could do this, without ever giving it a try."

He fell into an exhausted silence.

"Marsha, I love you," he said, finally, with surprising gentleness. "I just have to do this. If it doesn't work out, I promise you I'll go back to medicine."

She tried to accept it. She said she would come to New York with him to look for an apartment. But when she got there, she found she hated the city. She did not think that it was fair to have to give up her beautiful house, schools for the kids, and friends. That was what was important to her. She tried to imagine living in New York, cramped in a small apartment, going back to work part-time, never seeing him because he would be working nights and going to school during the day. It was just too bleak.

"I love you," she told him, "but if you go to New York, you go alone, without me or the kids."

So he went to New York alone, lived in a studio apartment, and supported himself working nights in an emergency room.

Two years later the phone rang in my office. The voice sounded strangely familiar.

"Hello," it said, "this is Bob Orson. I'd like to come and see you again."

The acting career had not worked out. He was good at it. The operating room had never made him feel as alive as did parading the stage as King Lear or sinking into his chair as Willy Loman. But he could not catch up with those who had spent their college years debating the best staging for *Oedipus Rex* rather than memorizing hydrocarbon chains. Perhaps if he had tried it back then he would have learned for sure how he measured up compared to other aspiring young thespians. Now the best he could hope for, he realized, was a dedicated amateur status.

Bob returned to the suburban town where he had worked before and where Marsha and the children remained. He got a small apartment and began working in the emergency room of the same hospital where he had once shared the title of chief of ophthalmological surgery with his former partner.

"With acting out of my system, I feel a certain peace," he told me. "I want to return to medicine. But I'm not sure if that's what I should do. Before, I was clearly chasing rewards—money, status, power—but those have lost their grip on me. Without them, I'm not sure why I should be a doctor."

"What did you most enjoy about medicine?" I asked.

"Really, the same thing I enjoyed about acting: the applause of the crowd; the sense, however remote, of having an impact on others; and the feeling of power over their lives and emotions. But that's all gone."

"Bob, what now stirs in you when you imagine the world of examining tables, prescription pads, and operating rooms?"

"Not just helping people—there are lots of ways to do that. And not just making money either. I don't really know, and that's what bothers me."

"When you think about what makes something in your life meaningful, what ideas do you come up with?"

"Doing what I want."

"What does that mean, acting on your whims?"

"If I'd been asked that question five years ago and if I'd answered honestly, I would have said that being myself did mean acting on my whims and feeling more powerful than those around me. Having to stand on my own and then realizing that I blew it and that I wasn't going to make it plus all those hours of acting lessons taught me to respect and listen to myself. Those were such incredibly costly lessons; look at all the trauma I've caused myself and the people I loved—I lost Marsha and the kids over all that. I wish I had learned to listen to myself earlier in my life. But I guess it's better late than never. I guess those years in New York weren't a total waste."

"Why is that important to you, expressing yourself? How does that give meaning to your life?"

"My first reaction is that the question makes no sense. There is no meaning to life, there's nothing outside us that gives our lives meaning.

"But then I sometimes wonder, Why do medicine? Why worry about health and sickness? Why pay the tremendous costs of modern medicine to preserve so meaningless a thing as life?

"Sometimes I think that medicine has no meaning. It's a means to an end, it gets me what I want—money, status, power, lots of new toys. I tell myself to enjoy it or enjoy what I get from it. But I know if I go that route, I'll never have enough toys. I learned that it's really true: The more I have, the more I want, and so I never get enough. That's a prescription for chronic frustration and dissatisfaction. I won't go down that road again."

Bob paused for a moment.

"This is crazy," he said to me. "You're making me crazier, not saner. This makes no sense. How come I can ask all these questions I can't answer? Did evolution screw up? I always used to marvel at the complexity of the human machine. I am still in awe of its intricacies and the process that produced them. But this is crazy, to grow a species that can torment itself asking questions that have no answers. None of what we call the lower animals makes itself crazy. Maybe we're the dumb ones."

Driving home, Bob passed the hospital. Incredible, he thought, we've spent millions upon millions of dollars to keep a couple dollars' worth of chemicals breathing and thinking. The breathing goes nowhere, it's just going to stop one day, no matter what we do. Medicine is a losing game; death gets us all in the end. And the thinking does us no good either; it just makes us miserable.

When you're miserable you take a pill. Bob thought of Fred with his heroin; Petroski, the psychiatrist on staff who did line after line of cocaine each day; and Brodsky, the orthopedic surgeon, with his gambling junkets. Pushers! They're not healers, he thought in anger, they're pushers. Is that what medicine has come to? Not healing the sick but drugging them all into oblivion? Are we going to start thinking of living itself as an illness that we have to treat with morphine, Valium, Prozac? Is a physician now the moral equivalent of a street dealer?

No, he thought immediately, there's more to it than that. He remembered a dying man whose life he saved by a simple shot of penicillin when he was an intern, and the heart transplant he'd once watched, and the nearly blind to whom his surgery had given new sight. But why? That question returned to haunt him. A few more years of life, a few more minutes of happiness? Was it worth it? If happiness is all that matters, Fred and the others are right; we could make everybody happy by putting a few chemicals in the drinking water. Everyone would be blissed out all the time.

But would they be truly happy?

No! Bob shouted to his empty car. Stop! I can't take this anymore. I remember that question of what is real happiness from college philosophy. It drove me nuts back then; I'm not going to let it drive me nuts again. There are no answers. Face it. I'm in the top IQ bracket, and if I can't find the answer, there's no answer, period. I have to find a way to shut off my mind. Millions of years of groping evolution to produce the human mind, and this is what those millions of years have come to—me, one of the brightest products of evolution, and all I want is to shut my mind off.

It was growing dark; the car was proceeding out of town. If he turned left now, he realized, he would be heading into the country, the hills and ravines. Suddenly the picture of his car plummeting over one of the ravines and bursting into flames flashed through his mind. No, a voice immediately said from inside, too bloody. Use the morphine back at the office. One big injection and you go out in bliss.

Without thinking, like a reflex, Bob's foot slammed on the brake. The car swerved to a stop. I can't believe it, he said to himself, here I am calmly thinking of killing myself.

That night I got a call from Bob. I told him to come and see me first thing the next morning.

"I can't believe the conflict," Bob said to me as soon as he was settled in my office. "The last thing I want to do is die, but when I shift the burden of proof—as my debate coach used to say—to the question of *why live*, it's a shock to realize

I have no really good answer. One voice inside says there must be more to life than 'Eat, drink, and be merry,' or else nothing makes any sense. Another voice says I'm just a coward and can't face the fact that nothing does make sense. And another voice says, Forget it—eat, drink, and be merry. And so I go around and around in circles."

"Bob, you're treating this like it was a problem in diagnosis. You're saying to yourself, If I just think hard enough, the answer will come to me. But it's not the kind of problem that can be solved by hard thinking alone. Hard thinking may be part of the solution, but it's probably not the whole answer."

"What else do we have? Reason is the crowning achievement of evolution."

"Bob, I want you to relax and picture your favorite scene. Then in your mind's eye, I would like you to construct a dwelling there, a place you would like to go for relaxation and self-reflection. Furnish it any way you wish. Build into it whatever you need or want."

His mind rebelled. "What kind of mumbo jumbo is this?" he demanded. I sensed the discomfort behind his words.

"Think of it as an experiment, a way of gathering data."

After a while Bob relaxed, closed his eyes, and envisioned a small cabin in the woods. Only a few rooms. A kitchen at one end of the living room, with a large fireplace at the other. A library with hundreds of volumes. A small bedroom.

"Very ascetic," I said, "and rather lonely, no?"

"Yes, but it will do for the moment. For now I simply want to be alone. No more audiences, no more medical groups. I just need to be alone."

"Now picture yourself entering your cabin. Sit there in a comfortable way. Feel yourself becoming more and more relaxed there. What emotions are you experiencing—peace, joy, fear, calm, awe, anger, anxiety, emptiness, love? Don't try to do anything with these feelings now, just sit with them and let them pass through you. Spend a few minutes in your relaxed state, reflecting on the experience. Then gradually return to ordinary consciousness. Please keep some notes on this experience."

After a few minutes Bob opened his eyes and said, "That's crazy. This is too much."

"What happened, how far did you get?" I asked.

"Well, it was hard simply to envision that room. It just confused me. I'm a man of science, remember, not an ex-hippie."

"But you're also a human being. I'm not asking you to believe anything on faith. I'm asking you to discover parts of yourself you've lost touch with. Treat this suggestion like an experimental hypothesis, something to be confirmed or disproven by experimentation. Only here the subject of the experiment is yourself. All I'm asking you to do is to experiment in a disciplined way, just like you do in the laboratory.

"And, like all human beings who take the time to reflect on themselves—you yourself said the capacity to do that separates us from the animals—you have questions about yourself and the meaning of your life. Questions that, as you have learned from your own experience, can't be answered by simply thinking intently. I want you to continue to learn from your experience. Discovering another part of you is the first step in answering those questions. Do you want to try it?"

"But how does that cabin-in-the-woods exercise help?"

"I don't know. I know it's worked in a powerful way in the lives of those who have practiced it with discipline. But I understand your skepticism. I am skeptical too. Especially since I can't explain how it works. But there are a lot of things I don't understand—more things out there than are dreamt of in your and my philosophy, so to speak. I know only that people who work with it regularly report many changes in their lives, and you will too."

So Bob wrote down the instructions. That night after work, he had no trouble envisioning his place of retreat in the woods. But not much else happened.

"It's not working," he told me over the phone. "I guess I just don't have a soul."

"Sounds to me like you are trying to make something happen. I didn't ask you to try to imagine what your soul looks like. I asked you to be quiet. Don't try to picture something, just see what comes."

Bob was expecting a vision of some being of light, some angelic, glowing figure. Instead he fell asleep and dreamed that a stocky, bearded man in a plaid flannel shirt, jeans, and work boots knocked on the door of his cabin. Later he would recall it as one of the most vivid dreams in his life.

"Who are you?" Bob asked the man. "I expected a god or an angel."

"And you, the atheist, thinks he knows what gods and angels look like?" the man said with a gently ironic tone.

"I didn't think he would look like Paul Bunyan," Bob replied.

"But you must have, since your mind created this image, or so you think."

"Of course my mind created it. It's my imagination."

"Of course, just like any dream. You create all your dreams too, don't you?"

"Of course."

"That's why you always know what's going to happen and understand what they mean," the woodsman said in that ironic tone again. "If something happened that you had no control over and didn't understand and oftentimes didn't want to, would you say that event was your creation?"

"No," Bob admitted.

"But that's what happens in the case of dreams, and that's what's happening with me too. In what sense, Doctor, am I just your creation?"

"But where else would you come from if not my mind, at least my unconscious mind?"

"I thought you didn't believe in the unconscious," the man said, alluding to Bob's ongoing arguments with two of the psychiatrists at the hospital.

"I don't know what I believe anymore."

"That's good," the woodsman said, "don't believe anything. Stick close to experience. At least at first."

After a pause, the bearded man said, "Well, I have to go for now. But you may see me again."

The dream ended and Bob found himself sitting on the sofa in his apartment, bewildered but intrigued. I wonder what more he had to say, Bob thought. But that's crazy; why don't I know, since he's a creation of my mind?

The next evening Bob sat on his sofa, closed his eyes, and relaxed. Again he drifted off and dreamed of his cabin, of the woods, and then of a bearded man in overalls and work boots sitting in a chair.

"Who are you?" Bob asked.

"Who do you want me to be?"

"I don't know, some kind of wise man who will answer my questions."

"Ah, a guru. I've heard you be pretty sarcastic about gurus and swamis and fortune-tellers."

"Is that what you are?"

"That's what you said you wanted me to be. How could you want me to be something you despise? Except that would make it easier to dismiss what I say."

"How come you seem smarter than I am?"

"When I'm only a figment of your imagination," the portly bearded figure added, finishing Bob's thought.

"Yeah, when you're only a figment of my imagination."

"Maybe that's not what I am."

"Then what are you? Here we go around again. Quit playing games with me."

"I thought you liked playing mind games, Doctor. You always liked to debate. Sometimes you'd take a position just to argue, although what you really wanted to do was show how smart you were."

"You know me so well," Bob said sarcastically. "You're right, I used to do that, but I don't do that anymore. Now, are you going to tell me who you are?"

"Fair enough, I'm a teacher."

"Ah, so you will answer my questions."

"What questions?"

"Since you know everything about me, you surely know what questions?"

"I thought you said you gave up mind games. Why is it so hard for you to admit the kinds of questions troubling you? Why do you feel like it's confessing a crime rather than just accepting the fact that you have these questions?"

"It does feel like a crime, a crime against reason, against reality. In reality there is no answer to these questions."

"True, not in the reality you know. But how do you know that's the only reality?"

Again a pause and then the figure said, "I have to go now; I assume I'll see you later."

Bob awoke in the middle of the night alone in his living room with the last question echoing in his mind: How do I know that the world of sticks and stones and chemical reactions is the only one? He sat up, undressed, and crawled into bed. The question was on his mind on the way to work and would pop into his head every time his mind was unoccupied.

A few nights later he dreamed again of the bearded figure.

"Well, did you come up with an answer to the question I left with you?" This time the bearded man began the conversation.

"No. But you're supposed to answer my questions, I'm not here to answer yours."

"Who says?"

"But I got into this because I wanted answers to my questions. What's the purpose of all this if you're not going to give me an answer?"

"Have you learned anything from our discussions so far?"

"Yeah, a new meaning for the term *confusion*. Confusion is when you argue with yourself and you lose."

"Very good. Confusion is a symptom of the fact that there are things you don't understand. And that's the truth, there *are* things you don't understand. Understanding that is the beginning of understanding."

"What a crock of b.s.," Bob said angrily.

"Perhaps. But it still may be true. What makes you so angry about there being things you don't understand?"

"I don't know; but you're right, the idea infuriates me."

"You have to know everything?"

"Of course not; I'll never understand nuclear physics or what Sophocles had in mind when he wrote *Oedipus Rex*. There are lots of things I'll never know, but all of those things are knowable by someone. What I don't like is the idea that there are some things that just can't be understood, period."

"Mystery. Mystery makes you furious. The idea of something that's real and important but incomprehensible, and that you just have to live with the mystery of it, is an affront to you."

"Exactly. It's an affront to human rationality."

"What would it mean, though, if it turned out to be true that human reason was limited? A good instrument within certain limits but not the answer to all questions."

"But it's all we have."

"It's all you have."

"What else is there but superstition?"

"Very simple, very neat—only two choices, reason and superstition. Everything you can't understand gets branded superstition. Certainly does simplify life. Probably makes you feel safe and secure too in your neat and tidy world."

The bearded figure's irony had turned to open sarcasm. Bob was shaken by the biting tone of his words.

"Oh," the woodsman continued almost like a fighter smelling a kill, "you can dish it out, but you can't take it? I've heard you be even more cutting about ideas you dismiss as silly. What's wrong, can't take your own medicine, Doctor?"

Before Bob could reply, his inner antagonist abruptly changed tone. "Just imagine for a second that there truly were realities beyond the scope of your present set of ideas. What would that feel like?"

"The idea makes me crazy."

"Crazy how?"

"The word that comes into my mind is control. To understand is to control. If there's something I can't understand, it means there's something I can't control. Then the world is out of control, everything is arbitrary and capricious."

"Again, very black and white, either total control or total chaos, totally comprehensible or totally meaningless. So the only thing you can trust is yourself, your ability to be in control."

"Of course, there's nothing else to rely on."

"And when you feel you're losing control, as you have the past few years as your life has gotten more complicated, of course you feel angry and crazy. In your mechanical world, in which everything is orderly and predictable, complexity and mystery have to feel like insanity."

"Hey!" Bob said angrily, "That mechanical world has given me tremendous power and prestige and a sense of being in control."

"True. But there's more to life than that. And that's what you can't accept."

"Yes, that's exactly right. I don't think I can give up control."

"No one gives up control. You can't will to turn off your will. But the complexity of life often wrests control from us. We don't give it up, we fight to keep it. That's why change involves so much suffering."

Unexpectedly the figure waved his hand, and in his dream Bob felt himself transported from his cabin to the shore of a lake. Actually Bob recognized the scene as an actual lake in a state park about half an hour from his house. He was sitting by the shore, surrounded by pine trees, totally absorbed in the scene. A strange calm settled over everything, and Bob couldn't tell if the calm was outside him or inside. Suddenly the distinction made no sense. He felt pulled down into that calm, and he sank into a deep, deep sleep.

When he awoke, in the middle of the night, the picture of the lake shore and the feeling of calm seemed permanently etched in his mind.

The next day he rearranged his schedule, left work early, drove to the state park, and hiked the two miles into the lake. It was just like the scene in his dream. Sitting on the ground with his back against a pine, the same overwhelming feeling of calm engulfed him. The next thing he knew, it was dusk; he had been there two hours.

At least once a week, Bob hiked back to the spot and settled into that peaceful state. Other days, before he went to bed, he would recall the scene in his mind and the same peacefulness would come over him.

As he did that, Bob began to notice changes in his life.

No dramatic conversions, no life-changing moments, just a gradually dawning realization that things looked and felt different.

I understand all the chemistry and biology that makes up me and these plants, Bob thought one day by the lake. But the beauty of it, the impact of it on me, I'm not sure where that comes from. *Hamlet* is only ink on a page, but when I speak those inky words before an audience, something happens between them and me that goes beyond just words and scenery and lighting. Beethoven's Fifth is but vibrations in the air, but those vibrations evoke an experience beyond just the wind blowing the air, an experience in which time stands still and that leaves me stronger than I was before. Strange chemicals, Bob thought, that produce not just reactions but experiences.

MARSHA AND the children had stayed behind in their house when Bob left. The children's playmates were there, and Marsha had wanted the support of her circle of friends in the community. While in New York, Bob tried to see the children, but the demands of lessons and practicing every day and emergency room work on the weekends left him little time to travel home. He had probably seen his children only every other month when he could get a weekend off.

Back in town he began to take them out to dinner every Wednesday night and to see them every weekend. At first his times with his son and daughter—now in preschool programs—were strained and tense. But Bob, understanding their confusion about his coming and going, persisted in taking them out. Gradually they all found they enjoyed playing board games on the floor of his apartment and going into New York on weekends to visit the zoo or to see children's theater.

Back home, Bob was content to work in the emergency room with the toughest cases. It brought back something of the challenge of his earlier days in medicine on the frontier of ophthalmological surgery. At first his old colleagues turned away when they passed in the hall. But gradually the other physicians came to respect his dedication and competency and began to call him in on consultations involving eye diseases. He had no desire to go back to competing for a chief's position or a department head. Yet neither did he want to waste his training.

A group of general practitioners had an unused office in their suite and let Bob rent it on a daily basis. Gradually he got back into the practice of ophthalmology, doing some specialized surgical work in conjunction with a more general practice.

Mariann had been the nurse in the office when Bob was in practice before. By coincidence she had left shortly after he did to have a child. She was looking for a part-time job just as Bob was starting back into practice, and he hired her. As they were locking up the office one night, a young woman appeared with a boy, his head wrapped in a towel.

"Are you a doctor?" she asked desperately.

"Yes he is," Mariann answered for him, "but the office is closed; take the boy to the hospital emergency room."

"But he says he got poked in his eye and he can't see, can't you help me?"

Bob knew time was crucial, too much time might already have passed. But he was not set up to operate.

"I would see him, but I'm not ready for surgery."

"I'll stay if you want," Mariann said quickly. "I'll just call the sitter."

My God, Bob thought, it's not just a job to her. His mind flashed back to all the times she had stayed late in the old office, or called patients to follow up on her own. Neither he nor his partner had bothered to thank her.

When the surgery was done and the boy sent home, Bob turned to Mariann, thanked her for staying, and apologized for the past times when he hadn't. She looked surprised, mumbled "Thank you," and walked through the door. Suddenly she turned and looked at Bob directly and said, "You really have changed. You really are a different person since you've been back."

Changes. Small changes. A contentment walking by the lake shore. An ability to look at his children, his patients, his co-workers with softer eyes and see a new beauty in them. The courage to tell them what he saw in them and to listen to what they saw in him. The realization, growing quietly within him, that there was more to life than the chemical machinery of medical school science and the will to power that drove through his medicine and his acting.

And Bob panicked.

"If there's something greater beyond me, how will it affect me?" Bob asked in desperation. "Will it control me?"

"You can't win, can you?" I said. "You want something to be out there to give your life meaning, but when you get near it, you don't want it."

"What will it do to me, swallow me up? Control me?"

"Bob, just because you see everything in terms of being in control doesn't mean that the whole universe is organized that way."

"I don't know anything else. I don't know any other way to think."

"I want you to deepen your experience of that panic," I said, "while remaining calm. Let it wash over you. Ask yourself, When have I felt this way before? When did I first feel this way? What thoughts and images come into my mind when I feel this way?"

Bob saw himself in a jail cell, bars on the windows, chained to a cinder-block wall. Suddenly the wall started moving toward him, closing in on him. The space got smaller and smaller. He felt the panic rise in his stomach and tighten his throat.

Suddenly he sat upright in the chair, eyes wide open.

"I can't do it," he said to me, "I can't go through with it. I'm too scared."

"You have to go through with it. There's no turning back. Go back and recall the image."

Bob was once again chained to the wall, only now the walls had moved closer together and the cell was hardly the size of a phone booth. The moving wall quickly covered the window, and all was dark. He couldn't even see the wall moving closer. But he knew it was coming.

Suddenly he felt it inexorably touching his toes, grinding his feet into the back of the cell. He screamed and blacked out.

Later he told me, "When I think of closeness, I feel claustrophobic, confined. And loss of control. Just like in that fantasy. I lose all control and get the life crushed out of me."

"Bob, go home and practice this over and over. Really sink into the fear, panic, disorientation, uncertainty that you feel, and let the images and thoughts that go with them run their course. That's the secret of doing this: hanging in there with yourself and seeing it through to the end."

"My whole life I've felt this way," Bob said the next week. "We've talked about that. I never realized how I felt controlled all my life. Everyone said, Be a doctor! So I became a doctor. Everyone said, Make money! So I made money. Everyone said, Be a success! So I was a success. But then I couldn't take it anymore. So I dumped the whole thing. But that didn't work either."

"Are those the only choices: either give in or break out?"

"But that's all I can think of. Relationships mean being either controlled or abandoned; so I leave first."

"But is that really true now? Is that the kind of relationship you have with your kids? Is that the kind of relationship you and I have?"

Bob thought about those questions on the way home. Maybe it was possible with another person, but with a God? Isn't that God's job, to be in control? Even with another person—it was hard to imagine there would be another person who did not want to control him.

"You've sure made a God in your image," I said to Bob at our next session. "Look at your own experience. You're not losing control over your life. You've taken more control over your life, especially your inner life, recently."

"It's true," he said. "When I'm in the woods I totally let go. I lose myself in nature. But when I'm done, I have not disappeared. In fact, I feel stronger. How can that be?"

He noted that this feeling of connection to nature was spreading to other parts of his life. Running along the lake, giving himself over to the pounding of his muscles. When he could do that, he ran his best. Or playing a part. When he immersed himself in a character completely and let that character act through him, he gave his best performances. Even his view of sex had changed. He had stopped trying to achieve something and just let himself go, concentrating on the other person. Lost—in nature, in ecstasy, in the role, in another person. Yet he never disappeared. As a matter of fact, these connections were when he felt most authentic.

Bob continued to take some time each day to sit by the lake, in imagery if not physically. Each time he would sink into the most peaceful state he had ever known: totally absorbed in his sense of connection with nature. While still intrigued at the intricacies of the biological machine, he began to sense, through the carbon rings and chromosomes, another presence. Perhaps, he thought one day, remembering the words of the novelist Thomas Hardy, nature really is but "one mask of many worn by the great face beyond."

CHAPTER 10

Speaking of God

THE LIVES of Tom, Bob, Marion, and others illustrate the renewal that comes when the grip of false selfhood begins to weaken and real selfhood starts to emerge, opening up new possibilities of connection to a sacred presence that gives life meaning and purpose. But their experiences of presence and power are not the end of the spiritual search; they are only another beginning.

AFTER DIVORCING her alcoholic husband and settling into her new responsibilities at work, Marion returned to college at night to finish her degree. Even though she was majoring in accounting to further her new career, the college required she take certain general courses. One was a course in philosophy. The professor spent much of the class ridiculing religion. He delighted in pointing out the conflicts he saw between the different religions. He never missed a chance to say that religious beliefs could not be proven or to illustrate the contradictions between certain religious assertions and common sense.

He was convincing. Marion learned that in some religions people worshiped statues, in others they killed people who worshiped statues. In some they practiced polygamy, in others they idealized celibacy. Religious leaders had once insisted in the name of their gods that the earth stood still or that women were inferior to men or that human sacrifice was all right. But Marion could not deny the experience of death and rebirth she had gone through, nor the powerful presence she often sensed as she walked in the woods or sat in the back of the church meditating on the cross or the statues.

When asked in class if she believed in God, she didn't know what to say. Before, she would have simply said yes. But she did not believe in the kind of God that was being satirized in her philosophy class. She had long since ceased to think there was an old man with a beard who sat on a throne somewhere up in space. It was easier to answer no, there was no old man in the sky. But saying she didn't believe in God didn't feel right either. The sense of presence remained. Sometimes she would ask herself if she was an atheist or a believer. She didn't know how to answer. Neither term seemed to fit her.

When the class was over, she stopped thinking about religion and God. It was too confusing. Without being quite aware of what was happening, she went to church less and less and took fewer contemplative walks in the woods. She was busy enough with work, school, and the start of a new relationship with a man.

She couldn't let go of her spiritual search completely. She found herself buying books on world religions and reading them. But the variety of different beliefs and practices just added to her confusion. She bought philosophical books on religion. They talked about God as another name for the universe, and that was too abstract for her. She bought devotional books, but most of them talked about God in masculine terms, and she just couldn't think of God as male. None of the ideas in any of the books she read appealed to her. What was left of her old beliefs? Nothing. She couldn't even tell whether or not she was an atheist. And yet . . .

And yet the sense of presence was still there. One day she was struck by the fact that her experience didn't need words. Words had not brought her back to life when she thought she was dying. Words did not give her the courage to break free of John's abuse and to confront her boss. Words did not comfort her now in her confusion. The wordless presence did. That experience was enough for her. After this realization she returned to the woods and to church, letting the familiar figures of Jesus and the saints and the phrases of the church service evoke that wordless experience, content simply to rest in that awareness.

THE WORLD'S religions contain a paradoxical affirmation. In different ways they all say that the Ultimate, God, is beyond words. The *Tao Te Ching* opens with the saying, "The Tao that can be named is not the eternal Tao." And we might also say, "The God that can be named is not the eternal God." But they also say that the Ultimate can be encountered through the words, rituals, symbols, images, and actions of these same traditions.

The reason for this is clear. All human language is limited and finite. Our languages develop out of our experiences within the bounded world of space and time. The insights we have are mediated through our neurological structures and cognitive systems and are expressed in the terms of our particular culture and history. Language is limited by space and time, culture, and individual experience. To speak directly about God is to limit God by treating God like an object in the world of tables and chairs. That is precisely what God is not.

This is the essential paradox of all religions. They must use finite, human terms to express what is essentially beyond all terminology. We need to be patient with the convolutions of religious language. It is trying to do something very difficult, if not impossible: to express what is ultimately inexpressible. We must use language, but we must not be trapped by it.

How, then, can we speak of God?

This question is especially difficult for us because our culture provides no culturally sanctioned way to speak about God or Gods or Goddesses. Our culture treats as "real" and of ultimate importance the existence of physical objects or the goals of economic policy. For these concerns we have publicly agreed-upon terms. When economists speak about the "rate of inflation" or lawyers allude to "due process" or physicists write about "elementary particles," even if we don't understand what they mean, we feel they are talking about something real. Because there is no commonly accepted language in which to discuss our ultimate questions, by contrast, speaking about what is sacred is considered private and idiosyncratic. When a theologian talks about God or a mystic speaks of the experience of the divine, we are inclined to treat these comments as private and subjective. Thus in this culture each of us is thrown back on our own resources to find our own ways of speaking about what is sacred to us. Any language we choose, therefore, will feel subjective and precarious.

Since God is beyond all categories, in one sense the answer to the question of how can we speak about God is that we cannot.

But if we can't speak of God, in what sense can we experience her? Or, more precisely, how can we experience that God is beyond speech? Some (like the nineteenth-century philosopher Rudolf Otto) claim that we can experience that God is beyond experience. Such a claim makes no sense. We cannot experience that something is beyond our experience. But are speech and experience so closely tied that we cannot experience what we cannot directly speak of? Remember the connection between knowledge and state of consciousness. Our ordinary speech is connected to our ordinary state of consciousness. But what happens to our ordinary speech in nonordinary states of consciousness? What would the experience of divinity being beyond human speech be like? We would experience (not just think about, but really *experience*) a passing beyond all our concepts of God. We would enter a state of consciousness in which our religious ideas and feelings were left behind.

For in the beginning it is usual to find nothing but a darkness around your mind, or, as it were, a cloud of unknowing. You will know nothing and feel nothing except a simple reaching out to God in the depths of your being. No matter what you do, this darkness and this cloud will remain between you and your God. You will feel frustrated, for your mind will be unable to grasp him. Learn to be at home in this darkness. Return to it as often as you can. . . . If in this life you hope to feel and see God at all, it must be within this darkness and this cloud.

This is the way such an experience is expressed in the fourteenth-century spiritual classic appropriately called *The Cloud of Unknowing*.

The same experience speaks through the contemporary writer Thomas Merton when he says, "In the deepest darkness we most fully" find God. But such states of consciousness are difficult, almost unbearable, for "we do not find it easy to subsist in a void in which our natural powers have nothing of their own to rely on."

Religions, creeds, practices, and traditions are built around certain images, ideas, or concepts. Each religious tradition is centered on specific core metaphors: "the ways of the Tao are effortless" or "reality is empty" or "the law of the Lord is just" or "God is love." Intellectually we know that the infinite is beyond any finite concept. But out of our need for security—for something to hang onto—we may cling to our familiar images of ultimate reality. Even the atheist clings to his concept of God's nonexistence. To pass through the cloud of unknowing is to have all these concepts wrenched away, to be left with nothing to cling to, to have no satisfactory way of speaking about or arguing against or grasping any source of security. This is an experience of tremendous loss.

Merton writes, "If we set out into this darkness, we have to meet these inexorable forces. We will have to face fears and doubts. We will have to call into question the whole structure of our spiritual lives." Later he calls this a process "that risks intolerable purifications, and sometimes, indeed very often, the risk turns out to be too great to be tolerated."

Inevitable limitations on our experience and expression mean that finally the divine can come to us only as the negation of all concepts. This tells us nothing about the nature of the Ultimate—which remains beyond our ken—only about our encounter with God, which must finally pass beyond language into a state in which concepts disappear into a void.

This experience cannot be cultivated or forced. Rather encountering the limits of even the most pious and orthodox languages occurs naturally as experience pushes us further and further beyond our ordinary ways of thinking and speaking.

And now you ask me "How shall I think about him, and what is he?" I have no answer. All I can say is "I don't know." Your question brings me into the same darkness and into the same cloud of unknowing that I wish you were in yourself.

This too is from *The Cloud of Unknowing.*

But how can the negation of all that is familiar be called an experience of God?

The prophet Elijah, according to the Hebrew Scriptures, was fleeing for his life and hid in a cave. As he waited there for God, a terrifying earthquake occurred, and the cave was almost demolished. But God did not come to him through this display of overwhelming force. Then a roaring fire erupted. But God did not come to him in that blaze of energy and light. And then a silence settled over the cave. English translations usually describe this as a "still, small voice," but the Hebrew more accurately says, "a silence so profound that it spoke." That's where Elijah encountered the presence of God. In a silence. A silence so deep that it spoke. Elijah, frightened and hiding in a cave, stood there trembling in the silence of God until it spoke.

For some today the voice of that silence is a woman's voice—the voice of the ancient Goddess. For others the voice that speaks is the voice of the God of Abraham, Isaac,

Jacob, Jesus, and Mohammed. Others hear the lilting songs of Krishna. For some the silence is its own voice, and they encounter the Absolute as the universal emptiness of the Buddha's teachings. But all these voices and realizations take place in the milieu of silence. All seek to express what is void of expression.

Joseph Campbell speaks of the "masks of God." But behind these masks is not a truer, more correct, image of the sacred. That would be just another mask. Behind all these masks is a void empty of all concepts and images! But here we have to be exceptionally careful. Emptiness is not just another, more correct, image.

I know many students who, in flight from the experienced tyranny or illogic of their Western image of God, become Buddhists. They say they are now atheists and believe in the emptiness of ultimate reality. But emptiness is not something to believe in. Emptiness is the absence of anything to believe in. It is neither atheism nor theism. In such westernized Buddhism, emptiness has been reified into a concept when emptiness is precisely what cannot be reified into concepts because it is the experienced death of all concepts. I am not talking about having the correct understanding of the idea of emptiness. I am talking about entering into the experience of the void. We may intellectually defend ourselves against this experience of emptiness, of negation, by turning emptiness into a concept that we can then discuss and debate and so protect ourselves from the actual encounter with pain and loss.

Ultimately whether we speak or not, we point to the void. If we speak of the God of Mount Sinai or the emptiness of Nirvana, we are not describing an object in the world of space and time but pointing to what cannot be encompassed in the categories of space and time because it encompasses all of them.

Herein is a certain freedom, a freedom that comes when everything has been lost, when virtually all intellectual baggage has been jettisoned. A freedom from all religious images; a freedom not to speak or to speak; to use imagery (knowing it is imagery) or not. For any speech we utter comes from the void and the state of unknowing.

The spiritual search is not only sweetness and light. Over the centuries men and women have found that when the mind is driven beyond its ordinary ways of thinking, it may eventually reach a point where it loses all its bearings. There is nothing to grasp or hold onto; there is no solid ground underfoot. This can be a lonely and terrifying experience.

For this reason, in our own day, Thomas Merton has written of calling into question the whole structure of our spiritual lives in a process that may become, at times, intolerable. And, centuries before, the author of *The Cloud of Unknowing* spoke of making ourselves at home in a state of darkness.

Even earlier, in the third century, Plotinus described the mind's solo flight into the unknown:

The mind reaching towards the formless finds itself unable to grasp anything for there is nothing to hold onto and in sheer dread of holding to nothingness the mind lets it go. This state is painful; often the mind seeks relief by retreating from all this vagueness to the region of sense, there to rest as on solid ground. . . . But this is the way of liberation from the alienation that besets us here . . . a flight of the alone to the Alone.

At the end of the fifth century an anonymous author known to us as Dionysius the Areopagite wrote a brief essay called the *Mystical Theology*. Dionysius suggests that since the divine is beyond all categories, God's existence can be neither affirmed nor denied.

Neither is He darkness nor light, nor the false nor the true; nor can any affirmation or negation be applied to Him. . . . We can neither affirm nor deny Him. . . . [The] Cause of all things transcends all affirmation, and the simple pre-eminence of His absolute nature is outside of every negation—free from every limitation and beyond them all.

Since the Age of Reason in the eighteenth century, our thinking about God has been dominated by the conflict of skepticism versus faith, atheism versus theism. This is a conflict over words. Important words. Holy words. But still just words. The divine is beyond words: beyond the pious words of the faithful and the cutting words of the skeptics. So we are left with nothing but that state of consciousness which is neither acceptance nor rejection, faith nor doubt. However, as Marion found out, in returning to this place again and again, we are gradually changed. For the point of entering the state of unknowing is not speculation but transformation.

What transforms us is not the categories we use or reject but the experience of entering the void. Any language, however pious or traditional, that defends us against the void becomes blasphemy. Any language, however abstract, erotic, or angry, that draws us into the presence of the void is holy.

Beyond the categories of emptiness and fullness, the sacred is not just pure vacuum. The Divine expresses herself through a variety of images without being identical with them. The speculations of the Upanishads and the image of the drop of water vanishing into the sea, the koans of Zen Buddhism and the lure of paradox, the heroics of Camus and

Sartre, the soaring calculations of Einstein whose God does not play dice, the grace of Jesus who forgives us our trespasses, the love of the Great Mother whose wisdom is read on the wind—all are permutations of the presence of the void.

The phrase "presence of the void" makes no sense, since we think that a void is what is absent, not present. But if the "present void" were only an empty absence, experiences of the void could not be empowering. Nor could they clothe themselves in the love of Jesus, the denunciations of Isaiah, the compassion of the ten thousand Bodhisattvas, or the wisdom of the Great Mother. The encounter with the "presence of the void" is never simply negation or despair.

The experience of emptiness is not itself empty. It is overflowing, leaving in its wake the seeds of wisdom and the power of the spirit. Such encounters are not given us as grist for speculative mills. They are given us so that, in returning to them again and again, we might dance and sing, break free from the procrustean limits of our culture, be empowered, grow in wisdom, like the disciples who were baptized in the Spirit and went from a depressed and dispirited group to a movement that redirected the course of world history.

The Disciplines of the Real Self

IN THE middle of this road we call our life, the hero of Dante's *Inferno* suddenly loses his way. A harrowing journey, from which he learns much, is required to bring him back to his life's path. Not everyone's journey of transformation is so dramatic. But, having seen many through their own process of learning and transformation, the following conclusions appear inescapable to me.

First, although it does not appear in everyone, the desire to know oneself to be connected to a larger, sacred source of meaning is a normal human desire and a regular part of one's development. Discovering such connections is often part of the solution to many of our deepest dilemmas.

Second, the same defenses that serve as barriers to being connected to our real self and to others also keep us disconnected from the sacred. When these barriers are broken through and the real self emerges, a sense of connection with or concern about the transcendent often surfaces.

Normally in this culture we see the world as a collection of separate objects contained within space and time. In this framework, questions about meaning and purpose make no sense. But they haunt us anyway, often driving us to therapists' offices. We have the potential to supplement this fragmented perception with a more unitive one by accessing that aspect of our self which experiences interconnection. To do so we must break through the defensive barriers we have erected against finding connections and recover the real self. This enables us to cultivate mature relationships.

Third, the steps we take in experiencing our relationship with the transcendent often parallel the steps we take in therapy to get in touch with our real self. These steps include confronting the maneuvers and feelings of the defensive selves; experiencing and grieving over the anger, pain, emptiness, loss, and other scars that marred the early years of life; and supporting new perceptions of ourself and others.

Tom had the courage to face the emptiness of his professional life. Bob confronted the inauthenticity of his choice of career. Marion came to terms with the ways in which her upbringing trapped her in a destructive marriage. All were rewarded with the capacity to make new choices more solidly rooted in their real selves. They also found themselves open to previously hidden parts of themselves and to an experience of connection to a greater reality. Bob discovered there was more to life and to healing than the elements in a test tube. Tom found a new meaning and direction to his life and work by immersing himself in nature and encountering a spiritual reality there. Marion's life was transformed as she was grasped by a wordless presence.

Fourth, this capacity for connection inevitably affects our entire life. Marion ended her marriage to John, setting him free to grow if he chose; she entered a more mutually engaging relationship and refused to play the victim at work. Bob left a high-status and high-pressure medical practice and shaped a new one characterized by a more personalized approach. Others change careers, contact estranged children, or become involved in community and religious organizations.

Service, then, is another way in which this sense of connection affects our lives. The connections explored in this book need to be expressed in action. They will atrophy if they remain locked within the individual psyche.

Usually this happens naturally: Having experienced connections, people spontaneously reach out to connect with others. Tom began to consult with struggling businessmen and started a newsletter to improve personal communication within the financial community. Many people I work with are already in a helping profession, but they report that their experience changes the way they relate to clients, patients, students, and co-workers.

When Kenneth, a sales manager, started to see me because of marital problems, his attitude was that to be a boss meant having iron-fisted control over his staff. The turnover was tremendous in his department, and those employees who remained tended to be the least productive who couldn't get jobs elsewhere.

He had been to various management development seminars but said he hated that "touchy-feely" stuff. In marital counseling he fought making any changes in his domineering style until his wife took their eight-year-old son and moved out. That same week he was given a critical job review and put on probation. Facing the loss of family and job, Kenneth summoned the courage to rk on himself. His wife, sensing a softening, agreed to come back to therapy with him.

It was a hard struggle for him to face the pain and rage and insecurity that fostered his need for such control. But the changes he went through affected not only his wife and son but spilled over into his treatment of his co-workers. He started to go out of his way to encourage each one and to find ways to enable each of his subordinates to do his or her best work. His image of being a boss changed from overpowering others to facilitating their accomplishments. His basic question shifted from Why the hell didn't you do better? to What do you need in order to do your best?

Service at home, at work, and in the community means simply expressing that sense of connection in action. While some people change jobs or undertake extensive community service, others, like Kenneth, do their jobs in a manner that reaches out to people and relates to them in new ways.

This reaching out is a means of expressing and deepening a new sense of connection. Such activity will not itself generate lasting meaning. It is a fruit, not a source, of new ways of relating. Many try to run from their emptiness and lack of intimacy by taking on a lot of projects. Many religious and civic organizations and well-intentioned advice-givers encourage this. While such hyperactive achievers may temporarily do much good in their community, they will end up empty, depleted, and burned out if this activity is a flight from themselves rather than an expression of themselves.

Still, a sense of connection cannot remain disconnected from others and shut up inside. A self-contained sense of connection is a contradiction in terms. It presses for expression in the public world. This need not be of heroic proportions. There are no stories here of people who leave home to serve in foreign lands or reduce themselves to poverty by giving everything away. This is a book about making connections, not a guide to solving all your problems, curing all your ills, or becoming a saint. But a crucial part of connecting your life to something beyond itself is to reach out to others.

Going through this process, then, people often realize that they are connected with other people, with nature, and with a universal and sacred presence. They learn that the real, personal self is grounded in a greater self or presence. This comes not as dogma to be accepted but as reality to be discovered and rediscovered throughout life.

And the connection they find is not the one they feared on the basis of childhood experiences or that they see played out in those religious groups that prey on a false selfhood. Mature spirituality is not slavery to a dictatorial power seeking the allegiance of compliant serfs or a smothering ocean pulling for a return to the symbiosis of infancy. Rather healthy spirituality grows out of individual, interconnected, and psychologically well established selves. Their communion with others and with God enhances rather than dissolves their identity.

The spirituality championed in this book is a spirituality of experience, the core of which is a lived sense of connection rather than rules, institutions, or doctrines. Its primary practice is a disciplined process through which each discovers his or her own connection with the sacred—a process that may take either traditional or nontraditional forms.

Commitment to and participation in mainline religious institutions has fallen sharply in America. The composite Princeton Index of Religion, put out by the Gallup organization to measure levels of religious involvement, has declined steadily every year from a high point in 1951. There has also been a continual decrease in expressed confidence in religion and religious leadership, which parallels the decline in public confidence in other institutions and leaders.

Yet this is only half the story. At the same time there has been a constant increase in the number of people who report they believe in God or some spiritual force (95 percent of the American population in 1991), who pray or engage in some spiritual practice (about three-quarters of the Americans surveyed), and who are willing to report a religious or mystical experience (slightly more than half of all Americans). Sales of religious books and subscriptions to religious periodicals and attendance at weekend religious workshops and retreats (all broadly defined so as to encompass everything from traditional Catholic catechisms to New Age visualization guides) have also steadily increased.

Contrary to the predictions of the nineteenth-century prophets of modernity who saw only the decline of religion, recent research portrays a virtually unprecedented, if somewhat chaotic, swirl of religious activity in the United States. Most of it occurs outside the walls of mainstream religious institutions. Thus a decline in church and synagogue membership has not meant a decline in religious interest. If anything, it has meant just the opposite.

Sadly, then, the search for spiritual connections often takes place outside the institutional life of religion. Many remain loyal to the faith of their forebears, but few find what they are looking for within those sanctuary walls. They are driven to look outside their traditions because often these religious forms do not resonate with the spiritual aspirations of present-day men and women or speak to their deepest longings for meaning. The connection with the Ultimate remains oddly disconnected from the forms that have carried that experience throughout human history.

Having found within themselves, or in nontraditional settings, the spiritual connections they were searching for, many men and women return to the traditions of their past. Like Marion, they now see in the traditional forms of speech and action meanings they have had to discover outside those traditions. Sadly, spiritual significance is often imported into churches and synagogues today rather than found there.

The forms of expression that people choose for their experience of communion with the sacred are virtually infinite. Some choose to express it through the most profound motifs of Judaism and Christianity, others through a kaleidoscope of metaphysical theories, others through the practices of the religions of the East, still others through images drawn from modern psychology, and there are many more besides. The experience of connection, as portrayed in this book, is what gives life to this wealth of religious expression.

I HAVE lectured on these topics for many years and have been constantly confronted with a misunderstanding. When criticisms of modernity are offered, people assume the next step is the advocacy of some authoritarian religion. This is indeed the precise ploy used by many religious hucksters. But the fact that this misunderstanding of my point often persists despite my attempts to correct it makes me wonder if something more defensive is not at work—perhaps the need to defend modernity's brittle autonomy or authoritarian compliance.

So for the last time let me state that my criticisms of modernity are criticisms not of science or technology but only of cultural and psychological styles predicated on them to the exclusion of everything else. The purpose of my discussion is not a return to authoritarian religious patterns (which I hope are sufficiently criticized in chapter 7) but just the reverse. I have provided tools by which each can discover his or her own connection with a larger reality that can give meaning and purpose to life.

Continuing the Search

OUR SPIRITUAL search does not end just because we have some kind of transforming experience. Such moments are only another step along the way. We continue to grow and to acquire new experiences. Our spiritual frameworks must expand to accommodate these developments. Often it happens that just as we think we finally understand the meaning of life or what is right and wrong, life serves us some event that sends us back to our spiritual drawing boards. Thus the themes of this book are the subject of a lifetime of practice and reflection.

Also, given my desire to reach as wide an audience as possible, there seemed every reason not to weigh down the text with footnotes. Some readers may be interested in the sources of the main ideas and quotations used throughout this book, as well as in the intellectual background of the points made here and some further reflections upon them.

Others may want material for further exploration. For all these reasons this bibliographical essay is provided.

INTRODUCTION

The quotation from Rilke is from *Letters to a Young Poet*, trans. M. D. H. Norton (New York: W. W. Norton, 1954).

The theoretical framework informing this book hardly originated with the author. Rather it stands in a long tradition of psychodynamic thought about human development and personality, and more particularly that strand of psychodynamic theorizing that is currently referred to as "object relations" theory.

What is original here is the application of the distinction between the real self and the false selves to understanding religious experience and the attempt to make that understanding available to men and women who are struggling with these issues.

Object relations theory represents a fundamental revision of psychoanalytic theory after Freud, which was carried out by several analysts in Great Britain. In Freud's biologically driven theory, the only motivation for behavior was the release of pent-up tension. The "object" of that impulse was of lesser importance. In object relations theory, by contrast, the need to establish relationships with others—not instinctual drives—is the primary human motivation. Our primary need is for relationships, and our personality is structured around the internalization of our relational experiences.

These interpersonal patterns are often re-created throughout a person's life. Over and over, in a variety of guises, we may find ourself fighting against a controlling father, being humiliated by a critical mother, pursuing a distant parent, or being the favored child of a doting grandmother. These same patterns may also be replayed in our religious life.

For more on object relations theory and the theoretical and clinical underpinnings of this book, see my *Contemporary Psychoanalysis and Religion: Transference and Transcendence* (New Haven, CT: Yale Univ. Press, 1991). The reader who is interested in exploring the interface of psychology and religion in more depth should consult this book.

Other authors have applied other aspects of the object relations model to the psychology of religion. Anyone interested in pursuing this inquiry further should also look at John McDargh, *Psychoanalytic Object Relations Theory and the Study of Religion* (Lanham, MD: Univ. Press of America, 1983); W. W. Meissner, *Psychoanalysis and Religious Experience* (New Haven, CT: Yale Univ. Press, 1984); Paul W. Pruyser, *A Dynamic Psychology of Religion* (New York: Harper & Row, 1976); and Ana-Maria Rizzuto, *The Birth of the Living God* (Chicago: Univ. of Chicago Press, 1979).

CHAPTER ONE

The quotation at the head of the chapter is from Carl G. Jung, *Modern Man in Search of a Soul* (New York: Harvest Books, 1933), p. 229.

The developmental research reported in this chapter is described in the following works:

Jean Piaget, *The Language and Thought of the Child* (Cleveland: World Publishing, 1955).

James Fowler, *Stages of Faith: The Psychology of Human Development and the Quest for Meaning* (New York: Harper & Row, 1981). The reader who is interested in exploring the developmental aspects of religion in more depth should consult this book.

Paul Ricoeur, *The Symbolism of Evil* (New York: Harper & Row, 1967).

For a somewhat more accessible treatment of some of the same themes, see Paul Tillich, *The Dynamics of Faith* (New York: Harper & Row, 1957).

Obviously, each of these topics—Piagetian theory, developmental research on faith and meaning, symbolism—is a whole field of specialization itself with host upon host of secondary studies and critical reviews. To attempt even a cursory review of any of them would be ludicrous and beyond the scope of this chapter. I simply want to point out that all of this research converges on the conclusion that the quest for meaning and a connection to the sacred is a fundamental part of human development.

I have suggested elsewhere that we are currently living in a time of major cultural transition beyond the ethos of modernity, as described in chapter 5 (James W. Jones, *The Redemption of Matter* [Lanham, MD: Univ. Press of America, 1984]; James Jones, "The Delicate Dialectic: Religion and Psychology in the Modern World," *Cross Currents* [1982]; James W. Jones, "The Lure of Fellowship," *Cross Currents* [1977]). Such a claim may be grandiose in the extreme, but it represents my understanding of the historical context in which this book is written.

The quotation from William James, regarding prematurely settling one's accounts with reality, is from W. James, *The Varieties of Religious Experience* (1902; New York: Penguin, 1982). This quotation neatly summarizes the procrustean tendencies of modernity.

One of the striking features of the revolution in physics that began at the turn of the century was the tendency among the physicists most responsible for these changes to devote the second half of their life to doing philosophy as well as physics. They attempted to work out the wider intellectual and human implications of their discoveries. The quotations in this chapter from the various physicists are found in Werner Heisenberg, *Physics and Beyond* (New York: Harper & Row, 1972), chap. 17; Erwin Schrödinger, *What Is Life and Mind and Matter* (Cambridge: Cambridge Univ. Press, 1969), p. 140; the quotations from Einstein are from Paul Tillich, *Theology of Culture* (New York: Oxford Univ. Press, 1964), chap. 9. For more on this topic, in addition to these books, you might also look at Werner Heisenberg, *Physics and Philosophy* (New York: Harper & Row, 1962); P. Schlipp, ed., *Albert Einstein: Philosopher Scientist* (New York: Tudor Publishing, 1951); E. Schrödinger, *Science and the Greeks* (Cambridge: Cambridge Univ. Press, 1954); James Jeans, *Physics and Philosophy* (Ann Arbor: Univ. of Michigan Press, 1958); and Carl G. Jung and W. Pauli, *The Interpretation of Nature and the Psyche* (New York: Pantheon Books, 1955). For a discussion of this revolution in scientific thought, see James W. Jones, *The Redemption of Matter* (Lanham, MD: Univ. Press of America, 1984).

Substantiation of the claim that having a sense of meaning and purpose in life is important for mental and physical health can be found in the following: Aaron Antonovsky, *Unraveling the Mystery of Health* (San Francisco: Jossey Bass, 1987); Aaron Antonovsky, *Health, Stress and Coping* (San Francisco: Jossey Bass, 1979); A. Bergin, "Values and Religious Issues in Psychotherapy and Mental Health," *American Psychologist* 46 (1991): 394–403; A. Bergin, "Religiosity and Mental Health: A Critical Reevaluation and Meta-analysis," *Professional Psychology: Research and Practice* 14 (1983): 170–84; K. Chamberlain and S. Zika, "Religiosity,

Meaning in Life and Psychological Well-Being," in J. F. Schumaker, ed., *Religion and Mental Health* (New York: Oxford Univ. Press, 1992); K. Chamberlain and S. Zika, "Religiosity, Life Meaning and Well-Being: Some Relationships in a Sample of Women," *Journal for the Scientific Study of Religion* 27, 3 (1988): 411–20; L. R. Peterson and A. Roy, "Religiosity, Anxiety, and Meaning and Purpose: Religion's Consequence for Psychological Well-Being," *Review of Religious Research* 27 (1985): 49–62; C. E. Ross, "Religion and Psychological Distress," *Journal for the Scientific Study of Religion* 29 (1990): 236–45; A. St. George and P. H. McNamara, "Religion, Race and Psychological Well-Being," *Journal for the Scientific Study of Religion* 23 (1984): 351–63.

The quotation from Ludwig Wittgenstein is from the final paragraph (Number 7) of his *Tractatus Logico-Philosophicus* (London: Routledge & Kegan Paul, 1955).

CHAPTER TWO

The accounts of spiritual experiences found at the end of this chapter are from F. C. Happold, *Mysticism* (New York: Penguin, 1963), chap. II.1. This is an anthology of religious experiences from a wide range of times, cultures, and religious traditions. The quotations in this chapter are all from twentieth-century persons.

The idea that spirituality involves our conscious relationship to our deepest self predates the rise of modern psychology, although psychology has given us a new language in which to understand this ancient idea. Plato and Plotinus both argued that the soul was a window on eternity and that through the contemplation of the eternal within us, we could glimpse that which transcends the sensate world of time and space. For more on this see *The Collected Dialogues of Plato*, ed. E. Hamilton (New York: Bollingen Foundation, 1963); *The Philosophy of Plotinus*, ed. J. Katz (New York: Appleton-Century-Crofts, 1950); A. E. Taylor, *Plato: The Man and His Work* (New York: Meridian Books, 1963); and R. T. Willis, *Neoplatonism* (New York: Scribners, 1972).

This idea was central to the work of two of the nineteenth century's most creative religious thinkers: Schleiermacher and Kierkegaard. Friedrich Schleiermacher defined faith as a form of self-consciousness—as our awareness that we do not create ourselves but are "absolutely dependent" on a power outside us for our existence—and made this definition central to his understanding of religion. See F. Schleiermacher, *The Christian Faith*, vol. 1, trans. H. Mackintosh and J. Stewart (New York: Harper & Row, 1973), introduction, chap. 1, part 1.

Søren Kierkegaard developed a model of the self as pure self-awareness which necessarily points beyond itself to a Source—a transcendent consciousness. Kierkegaard writes, in a sentence that might serve as a summary of the thesis of this book, that "by relating itself to its own self and by willing to be itself, the self is grounded transparently in the Power which posited it." In other words, as we both become aware of who we really are and choose to be who we really are, those actions point to the Power that is the source of the ability to know and to choose to be ourself. S. Kierkegaard, *The Sickness unto Death*, trans. W. Lowrie (Princeton, NJ: Princeton Univ. Press, 1941); the quotation is from part 1. Modern psychology adds to what has been said before a developmental understanding of that process of self-consciousness and a greater sensitivity to the way in which the pathologies of the psyche contaminate our knowledge of ourself and therefore also our knowledge of God.

Another important and obvious influence on this discussion of spirituality is Rudolf Otto's classic work on *The Idea of the Holy* (Oxford: Oxford Univ. Press, 1958).

There seems to be no end to the number of books available on a variety of spiritual practices. I have at least two shelves' full in my office. To discuss specific spiritual techniques and practices or even to review the significant books about them would require another book or books. That is beyond my scope.

For a general overview of the techniques and types of experiences and practices, see Daniel Golemen, *The Varieties of Meditative Experience* (New York: E. P. Dutton, 1977). Arthur Deikman, *The Observing Self* (Boston: Beacon Press, 1982) discusses one form of practice alluded to here in relation to psychotherapy and covers much of what I do here in more depth. The understanding of mantras and mantra meditation described here is based on Lama Govinda, *The Foundations of Tibetan Mysticism* (New York: Samuel Weiser, 1974). A more accessible introduction to Tibetan meditation can be found in Sogyal Rinpoche, *The Tibetan Book of Living and Dying* (San Francisco: HarperSanFrancisco, 1992).

For background on the discussion of the imperative element in science and religion and for more on science and religion as disciplines and systems of knowledge, see James W. Jones, *The Texture of Knowledge: An Essay in Religion and Science* (Lanham, MD: Univ. Press of America, 1981); Michael Polanyi, *Personal Knowledge* (New York: Harper & Row, 1974); and H. Rolston, "Methods in Scientific and Religious Inquiry," *Zygon: Journal of Religion and Science* 16 (1981): 29–63.

For background on the church fathers' view of the soul and the cosmos and the Stoic idea of the logos, see James W.

Jones, *The Redemption of Matter* (Lanham, MD: Univ. Press of America, 1984) and the references to Plotinus, Neoplatonism, and the church fathers above.

Our understanding of spirituality hinges on our model of human consciousness. The discussion of the status and nature of human consciousness has already filled many volumes—a process that shows no signs of slowing down. Even to list a part of that material would require another book.

Any discussion of consciousness will raise more questions than it answers. The following books and articles discuss human consciousness from a variety of perspectives. They provide some background for what is said here. And they will provide the interested reader with some of the information necessary to think these issues through on his or her own.

Alex Comfort, *Reality and Empathy: Physics, Mind, and Science in the Twenty-First Century* (Albany: State Univ. of New York Press, 1984).

Stanislov Grof, *Beyond the Brain* (Albany: State Univ. of New York Press, 1985).

James W. Jones, "Macrocosm to Microcosm: Towards a Systemic Model of Personality," *Journal of Religion and Health* 25 (1986): 278–90.

Lawrence LeShan, *The Medium, the Mystic, and the Physicist* (New York: Viking Press, 1979).

H. D. Lewis, *The Elusive Self* (Philadelphia: Westminster Press, 1982).

Richard Mann, *The Light of Consciousness* (Albany: State Univ. of New York Press, 1984).

Wilder Penfield, *The Mystery of the Mind* (Princeton, NJ: Princeton Univ. Press, 1975).

Roger Penrose, *The Emperor's New Mind* (Oxford: Oxford Univ. Press, 1989).

Coming to an understanding of the nature of consciousness is one of the most important things a human being can do, since to understand human consciousness is to understand human nature. A complete comprehension of consciousness may never be achieved, and there will almost certainly always be an element of "incompleteness" (in Goedel's sense) in every account of it. However, the very process of struggling with the question can give us new insight into ourself. Consciousness is something we all experience, and therefore we all have firsthand knowledge of it and can test any theories about it against our own experience. The books just listed are resources for the struggle, and spiritual practices are one way of probing its depths and coming to a direct understanding of consciousness. For both philosophical and scientific reasons, I argue against the currently popular hypothesis that consciousness can be completely explained in terms of brain functioning alone in J. W. Jones, "Can Neuroscience Provide a Complete Account of Human Nature?" *Zygon: Journal of Science and Religion* 27 (1992): 187–202.

Over the last decade there has been extensive research on the psychology and physiology of meditation. If you are interested in the array of scientific studies of meditation, you can consult the extensive bibliography found in Michael Murphy and Steven Donovan, "Bibliography of Meditation Theory and Research: 1931–1983," *Journal of Transpersonal Psychology* 15 (1983): 181–228.

In the simulation exercise described in this chapter, a group is asked to put themselves as completely as possible into the frame of mind characterized by modern science. Consciousness, freedom, and value are illusions, and life is a totally random and meaningless occurrence. I occasionally used this exercise in my courses on modern ethical issues. Still, students often failed to grasp the connection between this worldview implicit in modern science and the scenarios of meaningless violence and valueless hedonism that characterize much contemporary media drama and render ethical reflection virtually useless.

I assume it goes without saying that the purpose of this exercise is not to question the truth of scientific claims but rather to examine the impact of those claims on our life in the modern world. For my view of the truth of claims of science, see James W. Jones, *The Texture of Knowledge* (1981).

CHAPTER THREE

The distinction between the true self and the false self is rooted in the work of D. W. Winnicott. See D. W. Winnicott, *The Maturational Process and the Facilitating Environment* (New York: International Universities Press, 1965). The formulation of this distinction that I have found most helpful is that of James Masterson in *The Real Self* (New York: Brunner/Mazel, 1985). It is discussed in more detail in my *Contemporary Psychoanalysis and Religion* (1991). An insightful and evocative discussion of the concept of real selfhood is Christopher Bollas's *Forces of Destiny* (London: Free Association Press, 1989). In the present book I use this distinction in a much more religious way than is common in psychoanalytic circles.

Crucial to the argument of this book is the claim that our sense of self is created from internalized representations of our experiences of relationship. This claim is the core of all the object relations models of personality (cf. Jay Greenberg and Stephen Mitchell, *Object Relations in Psychoanalytic Theory* [Cambridge: Harvard Univ. Press, 1983]). Despite all the controversy in the psychoanalytic literature surrounding his work, Heinz Kohut provides what I consider to be the most helpful understanding of this theoretical framework (H. Kohut, *The Analysis of the Self* [New York: International Universities Press, 1974]; H. Kohut, *The Restoration of the Self* [New York: International Universities Press, 1977]; and H. Kohut, *How Does Analysis Cure?* ed. A. Goldberg and P. Stepansky [Chicago: Univ. of Chicago Press, 1984]). The focus on the importance of the emotional tenor of our early interactions and on our continuing need for affirmation, empathy, and emotional connection all reflect my immense debt to Kohut's work.

The developmental material used in this chapter is an amalgamation of several sources. As is obvious to anyone familiar with it, the most prominent source is the work of Erik Erikson (E. Erikson, *Identity: Youth and Crisis* [New York: W. W. Norton, 1968], and E. Erikson, *Insight and Responsibility* [New York: W. W. Norton, 1964]), which provides the overall framework for the understanding of human development used throughout this book. In my description of the developmental stages continuing through adulthood, each stage marked by the mastery of or failure at certain tasks, and my insistence that identity must precede intimacy, I have relied heavily on Erikson's formulations.

The material on the early years was taken from the work of Margaret Mahler (M. Mahler, F. Pine, and A. Bergman, *The Psychological Birth of the Human Infant: Symbiosis and Individuation* [New York: Basic Books, 1975]; and G. Blanck and R. Blanck, *Ego Psychology II: Psychoanalytic Developmental Psychology* [New York: Columbia Univ. Press, 1979]).

My concern about Mahler's theory, which I allude to in the text, is its one-sided preoccupation with individuation.

Perhaps this reflects its roots in classical psychoanalytic theory, which, especially in the case of Freud, continues and reinforces modernity's focus on atomistic individualism and the acquisition of individual autonomy as the goal of life. Titles like "separation-individuation" and "from symbiosis to individuation" carry the lopsided focus of a theory that ends with "object-constancy," the object relations equivalent of, and precondition for, psychic autonomy. Here Erikson seems wiser with his implication that development continues past adolescent autonomy into the capacity to reconnect and give oneself away in ever-widening circles of care.

Partly because it fits so well with the prevailing ideology of modern culture, Mahler's metaphor of development as a linear movement from symbiosis to autonomy has, I think, been taken overly literally by some psychological writers. It has also been severely criticized. Kohut, for example, who sees the self as continuously existing in a network of relationships, writes, "A move from dependency (symbiosis) to independence (autonomy) is an impossibility" (*How Does Analysis Cure?* [Chicago: Univ. of Chicago Press, 1984], p. 52). Another critique comes from the early infancy researcher Daniel Stern, who, in his book *The Interpersonal World of the Infant* (New York: Basic Books, 1985), cites evidence that the infant's experience is never symbiotic but is interpersonal from the beginning. Such findings relocate Mahler's schema in a larger context: A move from relative dependency to relative autonomy takes place in an interpersonal context. Autonomy, then, becomes a relational concept, which is one of the fundamental ideas of this book. Throughout this book when I refer to the process of separation-individuation, I mean it in this qualified sense. The dispute between Mahler and others for whom separation-individuation is basic and

Kohut, Stern, and others who rely on interpersonal models involves different primary assumptions about human nature. I discuss these issues in more detail in *Contemporary Psychoanalysis and Religion* (1991).

The suggestion that human development has a deep structure consisting of a pattern of going out and returning, in which autonomy is the task of the first half of life and intimacy that of the second half, is taken from Jung's conception of development. For a description of Jung's theory, see Edward Edinger, *Ego and Archetype* (New York: Penguin, 1973). This same pattern turns up in a wide variety of places. Plotinus, for example, sees it as the fundamental cosmic process, and Martin Buber describes it as central to the life of all relationships, including that of the self and God (M. Buber, *I and Thou*, trans. W. Kaufmann [New York: Charles Scribner's Sons, 1970]). In chapter 8 I suggest that this pattern is essential to any relationship—including the relationship to the sacred—in which real selfhood is maintained. That discussion in chapter 8 is clearly indebted to Buber.

CHAPTER FOUR

In keeping with my theme—that spirituality involves disciplined self-exploration—the vignettes in this book illustrate certain techniques of self-exploration that readers may use on their own. They are not necessarily verbatim transcripts of therapy sessions or examples of my therapy practice.

In working on the techniques described here for increasing a person's self-awareness and sensitivity to the inner processes, I was helped by the work of Eugene Gendlin, *Focusing* (New York: Everett House, 1978).

In my experience, imagery is one of the most powerful tools for increasing our self-awareness. There are many good books on the use of imagery. Readers having trouble getting started in this area might look at Arnold Lazarus, *In the Mind's Eye* (New York: Guilford Press, 1977).

The quotations from Buber at the chapter's end are paraphrases from Martin Buber, *I and Thou*, trans. W. Kaufmann (New York, Charles Scribner's Sons, 1970), pp. 158 and 159.

CHAPTER FIVE

The sociological background for the analysis of modernity in this chapter comes primarily from the following works: G. Simmel, *The Sociology of Georg Simmel*, ed. K. Wolff (New York: Free Press, 1964); Max Weber, *The Protestant Ethic and the Spirit of Capitalism* (New York: Charles Scribner's Sons, 1950), and Max Weber, *Max Weber: Essays in Sociology*, ed. H. H. Gerth and C. Wright Mills (New York: Oxford Univ. Press, 1946); Emile Durkheim, *The Elementary Forms of the Religious Life* (New York: Free Press, 1965), and E. Durkheim, *Suicide: A Study in Sociology*, trans. J. Spaulding and G. Simpson (Glencoe, IL: Free Press, 1951); Peter Berger, *The Sacred Canopy* (Garden City, NY: Doubleday, 1967); and P. Berger, B. Berger, and H. Kellner, *The Homeless Mind: Modernization and Consciousness* (New York: Random House, 1977). Major social theorists like Simmel, Weber, and Durkheim, and their contemporary descendant, Peter Berger, do more than describe the social forces and structures that make up modern culture. They also give an account of the impact of modernity on human life. Thus their work clearly has a moral and evaluative, as well as descriptive, dimension.

I have discussed these issues elsewhere myself in James W. Jones, "The Delicate Dialectic: Religion and Psychology in the Modern World," *Cross Currents* 32 (1982): 143–53; and

James W. Jones, "The Lure of Fellowship," *Cross Currents* 26 (1977): 420–23. The background of the discussion of the change in our view of nature can be found in J. Jones, *The Redemption of Matter: Toward the Rapprochement of Religion and Science* (Lanham, MD: Univ. Press of America, 1984).

The quotation at the head of the chapter is from R. Bellah, P. Marsden, W. Sullivan, A. Swidler, and S. Tipton, *Habits of the Heart: Individualism and Commitment in American Life* (Berkeley: Univ. of California Press, 1985), p. 286. Their surprisingly popular book covers much the same ground as this essay and should be read as further evidence for the understanding of modern culture alluded to earlier. However, given the strongly antipsychological and antipsychotherapeutic thrust of their book, I'm sure the authors of *Habits of the Heart* would regard my work as part of the problem, not part of the solution, and would see me as a symbol of much that is wrong with life in the modern world.

I have considerable ambivalence about *Habits of the Heart.* On the one hand, its central thesis certainly dovetails with my own. On the other hand, I clearly find their proposed solution psychologically naive, just as I suspect they find mine sociologically subversive. Fear of commitment is not simply the result of the social forces of modernity chronicled by Simmel, Durkheim, Weber, Berger, and the present authors. It is clearly rooted in the psyches of modern men and women and will not be overcome without a healing of the character defenses of the modern self.

Of course there is a sociological context to this dispute, and that is the long-standing feud between sociology and psychology over the relative weighting of intrapersonal and interpersonal factors in defining human nature. For more on this, see James W. Jones, "The Delicate Dialectic: Religion and Psychology in the Modern World," *Cross Currents* 32 (1982), and Peter Berger, "Toward a Sociological Understanding of Psychoanalysis," *Social Research* (1965): 26–38.

For a further discussion of *Habits of the Heart*, one can look at the spring/summer 1986 edition of the journal *Soundings*, which is dedicated to a symposium on this book with responses by Bellah and others.

At a deeper level, my essay attempts to go beyond this dichotomy between sociology and psychology. Modernity here represents both a constellation of social forces and a personal style characterized by a brittle, defensive autonomy and/or overly compliant and protean personalities. The ethos of modernity and contemporary personality styles are connected by the process of internalization and the construction of the self out of internalized object relations. I am proposing that through the process of internalization the cultural ethos is transformed into the structures of selfhood. Internalization, in which our experiences are incorporated into our developing sense of self, is the bridge between culture and the psychic life of individuals.

As the cultural ethos of detachment, control, and efficiency insinuates itself into family life, child rearing is increasingly governed by these same constraints. Then the child's early experience begins to resemble that of Harlow's paradigmatic monkeys. The emotional tenor of family relationships is the primary factor internalized, and the incorporation of an atmosphere of detached efficiency leads the offspring of modernity to develop false self structures. Their emotionally driven need for autonomy often hides deep, unmet needs for nurturance and dependency. This pseudo-autonomy affects their marriages and parenting and so is internalized by the next generation.

The allusion to Harlow's monkeys refers to a series of experiments by H. F. Harlow (for example, S. Suomi and H. F. Harlow, "Social Rehabilitation of Isolate Reared Monkeys," *Developmental Psychology*, 1972. The story of institutionalized infants given nourishment and shelter but little human interaction who ended up severely withdrawn and depressed, if not dead, can be found in René Spitz, "Hospitalism," *The Psychoanalytic Study of the Child* 1 (1945): 53–74 (New York: International Universities Press); and René Spitz, "Anaclitic Depression," *The Psychoanalytic Study of the Child* 2 (1946): 313–42 (New York: International Universities Press).

Another major problem I have with *Habits of the Heart* is that while the authors clearly advocate something they call community, they seem to me something less than clear in explaining exactly what they mean by community. Thus their book should be read in conjunction with others that discuss the nature of community in greater depth: for example, Robert Nisbet, *The Social Philosophers* (New York: Thomas Crowell, 1973), and Frank G. Kirkpatrick, *Community: A Trinity of Models* (Washington, DC: Georgetown Univ. Press, 1986).

There is, I hope, a clear theoretical model of human community and human relationships that stands behind my essay. Along with object relations theory, the other major theoretical framework that governs my understanding of the matters discussed here is general systems theory. Growing from the work of L. Von Bertalanffy (*General Systems Theory* [New York: Braziller, 1968]), general systems theory has had a wide application in psychology and psychotherapy (see, for example, W. Beavers, *Psychotherapy and Growth* [New York: Brunner/Mazel, 1977]). General systems theory focuses on wholes and organisms rather than on individuals or isolated parts. So, for example, living cells are understood in terms of their organization and function rather than in terms only of separate chemical compounds; or a family is understood as a single system with various members playing interrelated roles within the organization of the family rather than as a collection of separate individuals.

My own understanding of the scientific basis of general systems theory, rooted more in physics than in biology, can be found in J. Jones, *The Redemption of Matter: Toward the Rapprochement of Science and Religion* (1984). For my attempt to apply this framework to issues in psychotherapy, see James W. Jones, "Macrocosm to Microcosm: Toward a Systemic Model of Personality," *Journal of Religion and Health* 75 (1986): 278–90.

A major influence on my thinking about this matter has been the theoretical and clinical work of Salvador Minuchin, whose "structural family therapy" provided a means of translating my theoretical interest in the philosophy of systems theory into practical application. See S. Minuchin, *Families and Family Therapy* (Cambridge, MA: Harvard Univ. Press, 1974), and L. Hoffman, *Foundations of Family Therapy* (New York: Basic Books, 1981).

After having worked much of this out on my own, I came across two articles by Martha Crampton that develop the same paradigm used here. See M. Crampton, "Psychosynthesis," *Handbook of Innovative Psychotherapies*, ed. R. Corsini (New York: John Wiley & Sons, 1981), and M. Crampton, "Organismic Process: A Paradigm for Freeing Human Creativity," in *East Meets West: A Transpersonal Approach* (New York: Quest Books, 1981). The obvious congruence between what she was saying and what I was thinking was a great support to me at the time.

CHAPTER SEVEN

The psychological criticism of religion and its role in the dynamics of guilt and anxiety has a long history going back to Freud (S. Freud, *The Future of an Illusion* [Garden City, NY: Doubleday, 1964]) and Jung (C. G. Jung, *Psychology and Religion* [New Haven, CT: Yale Univ. Press, 1938]). It has been carried on more recently by Fromm (Erich Fromm, *Psychoanalysis and Religion* [New Haven, CT: Yale Univ. Press, 1950]) and Allport (Gordon Allport, *The Nature of Prejudice* [Cambridge, MA: Addison-Wesley, 1954], and Gordon Allport, *The Individual and His Religion* [New York: Macmillan, 1950]). And, in a way similar to what is done here, by Pruyser (P. Pruyser, *A Dynamic Psychology of Religion* [New York: Harper & Row, 1976] and *Between Belief and Unbelief* [New York: Harper & Row, 1974]). The purpose of these critiques varies widely. Freud saw his work as debunking religion and contributing to its demise. Jung and Allport saw their work as supporting religion, and in their own way so did Fromm and Pruyser. I trust it is clear that I intend my comments to stand in the latter camp.

CHAPTER EIGHT

The quotation from Buber is a paraphrase from M. Buber, *I and Thou*, trans. W. Kaufmann (New York: Charles Scribner's Sons, 1970), p. 165.

CHAPTER TEN

This chapter draws on the tradition of "apophatic" spirituality or the "Via Negativa," the so-called negative way, which approaches the divine through the negation of our ordinary concepts. This tradition of spirituality has particular relevance to the modern age, first, because today we have no theory of language that can support the direct ascription of our words to God. To speak directly of God was traditionally called the "Via Positiva," or positive way, in contrast to the Via Negativa. Such direct reference to God presupposes that human language can extend, at least by analogy, to the transcendent like Jacob's ladder reaching up to heaven. Our modern understanding of language, following Hume and Kant and other philosophers of the Age of Reason, is that human language is limited and finite and so cannot apply directly to any reality beyond the finite, physical world. Rather than argue against this skeptical understanding of language, the Via Negativa begins from a similar notion of the limits of human speech. But it goes beyond such a philosophy of language to focus our consciousness on the *experience* that remains once our awareness has passed beyond words.

Second, apophatic spirituality is especially relevant to the contemporary search for God because it recapitulates the history of religious belief in the modern period. Western culture, and, increasingly, non-Western cultures reached by Western technology, moved from a premodern culture of belief and dogma to a period of skepticism and atheism represented by Marx, Freud, Nietzsche, and others. These prophets of atheism assumed that with the rejection of literal dogma would come the end of all religion. But the Via Negativa insists that beyond the rejection of creeds lies not atheism but a new experience of the divine who is beyond all statements. The *experience* of the divine who is, in the words of Dionysius the Areopagite, "beyond affirmation and negation" moves us past the modern dispute of theism versus atheism, a dispute conducted as though those were the only alternatives.

Excellent brief introductions to apophatic spirituality can be found in Kenneth Leech, *Experiencing God* (San

Francisco: Harper & Row, 1989), chap. 6; the introductory commentary in F. C. Happold, *Mysticism* (New York: Penguin, 1963); and Andrew Louth, *The Origins of the Christian Mystical Tradition* (Oxford: Oxford Univ. Press, 1981). The philosophical background of this way of understanding and approaching God is discussed in John Peter Kenney, *Mystical Monotheism: A Study in Ancient Platonic Theology* (Hanover, NH: Univ. Press of New England, 1991).

Readers who want to explore further the topic of religious experience, especially in the Christian tradition, should consult Leech, Happold, and the writings of Thomas Merton cited below.

Classic Western expressions of this theology are the *Enneads* of Plotinus, *The Mystical Theology of Dionysius the Areopagite*, and *The Cloud of Unknowing*. The most powerful contemporary expression is in the writings of Thomas Merton, especially *Contemplative Prayer* (London: Darton, Longman & Todd, 1980) and *New Seeds of Contemplation* (New York: New Directions, 1961), from which the quotations in this chapter are taken.

The translations in this chapter from the *Enneads* of Plotinus (VI.9) are based on *The Enneads*, trans. S. MacKenna (New York: Penguin, 1969); and the critical text found in *Plotinus*, ed. and trans. A. H. Armstrong, Loeb Classical Library (Cambridge, MA: Harvard Univ. Press, 1966–88); and the translation found in J. P. Kenney, *Mystical Monotheism* (1991). The quotations from *The Mystical Theology of Dionysius the Areopagite* are from the version found in F. C. Happold, *Mysticism* (1963). The quotations from *The Cloud of Unknowing* are based on *The Cloud of Unknowing and the Book of Privy Counselling*, ed. William Johnston (New York: Image Books, 1973); and *The Cloud of Unknowing*, ed. James Walsh,

Classics of Western Spirituality (Ramsey, NJ: Paulist Press, 1981).

A further discussion of Otto's understanding and misunderstanding of religious experience can be found in my *Contemporary Psychoanalysis and Religion* (1991).

EPILOGUE

The fact that, in the last two decades, commitment to mainstream religious institutions has declined while interest in religion has remained stable or increased is supported by and discussed in more detail in the following: *Emerging Trends 1993* 15, 6 (Princeton, NJ: Princeton Religion Research Center, 1993); *Religion in America 1992–1993* (Princeton, NJ: Princeton Religion Research Center, 1993); Wade Clark Roof, *A Generation of Seekers* (San Francisco: HarperSanFrancisco, 1993); and R. Stark and W. S. Bainbridge, *The Future of Religion* (Berkeley: Univ. of California Press, 1985).